BHAGAVAD GITA - INSIGHTS FROM ADI SHANKARACHARYA

Bhagavad Gita - Insights from Adi Shankaracharya

DR SURABHI SOLANKI

First Printing, 2025

Contents

Preface

The *Bhagavad Gita* has been read, quoted, and revered for millennia, yet its message continues to reveal new dimensions with each era and each seeker. Among its countless interpreters, the voice of **Ādi Śaṅkarācārya** stands luminous — precise in intellect, fearless in inquiry, and unwavering in the pursuit of truth. His *Bhagavad Gita Bhāṣya* does not merely explain verses; it unveils the living spirit of Vedānta — that the essence of all existence is one indivisible reality, **Brahman**, and that realization of this truth alone liberates the human mind from sorrow and illusion.

This book, *Bhagavad Gita English: Insights from Adi Shankaracharya*, is an attempt to bring that timeless wisdom into the rhythm of modern understanding. My intention is not to translate Shankara's commentary verbatim, nor to dilute it with modern simplifications, but to **bridge** — to open a dialogue between classical Advaita philosophy and the contemplative seeker of today. The purpose is to make Shankara's insights accessible to readers who may not be scholars of Sanskrit or trained in traditional Vedānta, yet yearn for a direct engagement with truth.

Purpose and Approach

Every chapter of this work mirrors the original structure of the *Gita* and is accompanied by thematic reflections drawn from

Shankara's *Bhāṣya*. The verses are presented in translation, contextualized in their philosophical setting, and interpreted through the Advaitic lens. Alongside the doctrinal clarity of Shankara, I have included meditative commentaries that translate intellectual knowledge into experiential awareness — from *śravaṇa* (listening) to *manana* (reflection) and *nididhyāsana* (deep contemplation).

The approach is **scholarly yet experiential**. It respects textual accuracy while engaging contemporary language, ethics, and psychology. The aim is not to persuade but to awaken inquiry — for, as Shankara reminds us, true knowledge arises only when doubt dissolves in direct insight.

Audience

This book is intended for three circles of readers:

1. Spiritual seekers — those who wish to understand the path of knowledge (*Jñāna Yoga*) and integrate it with daily life.
2. Scholars and students of philosophy — who seek a faithful yet lucid exposition of Shankara's Advaita Vedānta.
3. Global readers — who may be new to Indian philosophy but are drawn to its universal wisdom beyond dogma or religion.

It is my hope that this work becomes a guide for introspection — not to teach what to believe, but to illuminate how to see.

Acknowledgment of Classical Commentaries

This endeavor stands humbly on the shoulders of great predecessors. I bow to **Ādi Śaṅkarācārya**, whose intellect and compassion forged the Advaita path with unshakeable clarity. I acknowledge the immense lineage of teachers who preserved and expanded his vision — from Sureśvara Āchārya and Madhusūdana Sarasvatī to Swami Vivekananda and modern Vedānta expositors.

This book draws upon authoritative Sanskrit editions of the *Bhagavad Gita Bhāṣya*, as well as English renderings by scholars such as Swami Gambhirananda, Swami Chinmayananda, and Swami Prabhavananda. I also recognize the contributions of modern academic interpreters who have brought Advaita Vedānta into contemporary discourse.

Yet, this is not a mere academic synthesis. It is a living reflection — shaped by the meditative insights that arise from reading the *Gita* as a dialogue within oneself: between confusion and clarity, between the individual and the infinite.

Closing Thoughts

Writing this book has been both a scholarly discipline and a sacred journey. Every page has deepened my conviction that the *Gita* is not a scripture of command but of realization — a mirror in which the seeker sees the Self as the Self.

As Shankara declares: *Brahma satyam jagan mithyā jīvo brahmaiva nāparaḥ* — "Brahman alone is real, the world is an appearance, and the individual soul is none other than Brahman."

May these pages serve as gentle guidance toward that recognition.

Love and reverence,
Surabhi Solanki
Uttarakhand
India

Introduction

Historical Background of the Bhagavad Gita and Adi Shankaracharya's Philosophical Position

The *Bhagavad Gita* stands as one of humanity's most profound spiritual dialogues — a scripture of revelation, reflection, and realization. Emerging from the heart of the *Mahabharata*, this 700-verse conversation between **Lord Krishna** and **Arjuna** transforms the battlefield of Kurukshetra into a theatre of consciousness, where the deepest questions of duty, identity, and liberation are addressed.

For centuries, sages, philosophers, and seekers have turned to the *Gita* for guidance through the moral and metaphysical dilemmas of life. It transcends the boundaries of religion, speaking instead to the timeless human struggle between confusion and clarity, action and contemplation, bondage and freedom.

The Historical Context of the Bhagavad Gita

The *Gita* occupies the sixth book of the *Mahabharata*, the *Bhishma Parva*. Scholars generally place its composition between the 5th and 2nd centuries BCE — a period of great intellectual and spiritual ferment in India. The Upanishadic insights into the nature of the Self had already taken deep root, and new systems of philosophy, such as Sāṅkhya and Yoga, were expanding their influence. The *Gita* arose as a **synthesis** — harmonizing diverse paths into a unified spiritual vision.

It presents three central modes of spiritual pursuit:

- **Karma Yoga** – the path of selfless action,
- **Bhakti Yoga** – the path of devotion and surrender,
- **Jnana Yoga** – the path of knowledge leading to realization.

The *Gita* thus became a practical scripture, transforming metaphysical thought into a way of life. It affirmed that realization is not confined to the forest hermitage but can be achieved amidst the duties of the world — a message of extraordinary relevance even today.

The Philosophical World Before Shankara

By the time **Adi Shankaracharya** appeared in the 8th century CE, Indian philosophical discourse had reached a critical juncture. Multiple schools of thought — Nyāya, Vaiśeṣika, Sāṅkhya, Yoga, Pūrva Mīmā�sā, and various strands of Buddhism and Jainism — competed to define truth and liberation.

The Vedānta tradition, based on the *Upanishads*, *Brahma Sutras*, and *Bhagavad Gita* (collectively known as the *Prasthāna Traya*), was fragmented by interpretive differences. Shankara emerged as a **unifying force**, restoring philosophical precision and scriptural coherence to Vedānta. Through his commentaries (*Bhāṣyas*), he clarified the metaphysical essence of the *Upanishads* and the *Gita* — proclaiming that the individual soul (*Ātman*) and the Supreme Reality (*Brahman*) are not two, but one.

Adi Shankaracharya: Life and Vision

Born in Kerala around 788 CE, **Adi Shankaracharya** lived only thirty-two years, yet his impact on Indian spirituality and philosophy remains unparalleled. A prodigious intellect and ascetic spirit, he mastered the scriptures at a young age and traversed the Indian subcontinent on foot — debating scholars, reviving monastic institutions, and establishing four *Mathas* (monastic centers) to preserve the Advaita tradition.

Shankara's mission was not merely intellectual but **existential** — to awaken humanity to the direct realization of the Self. He taught that ignorance (*Avidyā*) is the root of suffering, and knowledge (*Jnana*) alone dispels it. His Advaita Vedānta affirms a single, formless, infinite reality — *Brahman* — beyond birth, death, and multiplicity. The world, perceived as separate and diverse, is a superimposition upon that reality, much like mistaking a rope for a snake in the dim light. When the truth of the rope is seen, the illusion of the snake vanishes; similarly, when Brahman is realized, all duality dissolves.

Shankara's Commentary on the Bhagavad Gita

Among his commentaries on the *Upanishads* and the *Brahma Sutras*, Shankara's *Bhagavad Gita Bhāṣya* holds a special place. It is not merely an explanation of verses but a **spiritual map** guiding the seeker from ignorance to illumination.

Shankara interprets the *Gita* as primarily a scripture of **knowledge (Jnana)** rather than ritual or action. He recognizes *Karma Yoga* and *Bhakti* as preparatory disciplines that purify the mind and lead it toward insight, but he insists that final liberation (*Moksha*) comes only through **Self-knowledge** — the recognition that one's true nature is pure consciousness, eternal and unchanging.

In contrast to ritualistic interpretations that emphasize external duties, Shankara redirects the focus inward, teaching that renunciation is not of work but of the egoic sense of doership. This subtle but revolutionary insight transforms the battlefield of Kurukshetra into a symbol of inner awakening — the conquest of ignorance through understanding.

Philosophical Position: Advaita Vedanta

Shankara's system, **Advaita Vedānta**, is rooted in the threefold epistemological and metaphysical principles of:

1. **Brahman** – the ultimate, non-dual reality, beyond attributes and forms.
2. **Ātman** – the inner Self, identical with Brahman.
3. **Māyā** – the cosmic illusion that projects multiplicity upon the One.

According to Shankara, bondage arises from misidentification — when the infinite Self is mistaken for the finite body-mind complex. Liberation (*Moksha*) is not the attainment of something new but the **removal of ignorance**, revealing what has always been true.

He reconciles the diverse teachings of the *Gita* — action, devotion, meditation, and knowledge — by showing their progressive relationship. Actions (*Karma*) and devotion (*Bhakti*) prepare the seeker; meditation steadies the mind; and knowledge dawns as the final illumination.

Relevance for the Modern Seeker

Though written over a millennium ago, Shankara's vision speaks directly to the modern mind — a mind often torn between material pursuit and spiritual longing. His insistence on direct inquiry (*Vichara*), inner renunciation, and the realization of unity beyond difference offers not escapism but profound clarity in living.

In an age of information but little wisdom, his words remind us that knowledge is not accumulation but awakening — not an intellectual construct but a transformation of perception. The *Bhagavad Gita*, through Shankara's eyes, thus becomes not a relic of history but a living dialogue between consciousness and creation, self and society, action and awareness.

Conclusion

The *Bhagavad Gita* as interpreted by Adi Shankaracharya reveals the deepest secret of existence: the unbroken unity behind apparent diversity. To study it is not to learn something external but to remember what has never been forgotten — the truth of one's own Being.

As this book unfolds, it will follow the structure of the *Gita's* eighteen chapters, weaving together Shankara's insights with reflective commentary, to guide the reader from the turmoil of the battlefield to the stillness of the Self.

Structure of the Book

Division into Eighteen Chapters Aligned with the Gita and Illuminated by Shankara's Key Insights

This book follows the natural rhythm and design of the *Bhagavad Gita*, whose eighteen chapters trace the seeker's journey from confusion to clarity, from ignorance to knowledge, and from the finite self to the infinite reality. Each chapter represents a stage in the **inner evolution of consciousness**, and the commentary of **Ādi Śaṅkarācārya** acts as the guiding light through this journey.

To preserve both the philosophical integrity of the text and its spiritual accessibility, each chapter in this volume is organized into four consistent sections:

1. **Essence of the Chapter** – a concise summary of the original Gita teachings.
2. **Shankara's Vision** – exposition of the *Bhāṣya* (commentary) highlighting his Advaitic insights.
3. **Philosophical Commentary** – a modern exploration of how these insights apply to personal and contemporary life.

4. **Reflections for the Seeker** – contemplative notes or meditative exercises drawn from the spirit of Advaita.

The Yoga of Despondency

My limbs fail, my mouth is parched, my body trembles, and my hair stands on end.
O Krishna, I see ill omens; I cannot foresee any good in killing my own kinsmen in battle.
— *Bhagavad Gita* 1.28–31

The Battlefield of Consciousness

The *Bhagavad Gita* opens not with victory or divine revelation but with despair. On the vast plain of **Kurukshetra**, where armies stand arrayed for war, the warrior **Arjuna** — invincible in combat, noble in lineage — collapses in anguish. His bow slips from his hand; his heart trembles with confusion. The hero who had prepared all his life to uphold righteousness now finds himself incapable of action.

This moment of paralysis is not weakness; it is awakening. The battlefield here is both literal and symbolic — it represents the field of the human mind, where conflicting duties, attachments, and emotions wage their relentless war.

Arjuna's Inner Conflict

Arjuna's grief arises from the unbearable tension between **Dharma** (duty) and **Karma** (action). He must fight against his own teachers, elders, and kin — figures who embody his moral and emotional world. His question is universal: *How can right action exist when all choices lead to pain?*

In this crisis, the external battle transforms into an inner one — between the lower self, bound by attachment and emotion, and the higher self, seeking clarity and truth.

Shankara identifies this very conflict as the **first step of Yoga** — not the practice of postures or meditation, but the confrontation with ignorance (*Avidyā*). Only when the mind recognizes its own confusion does the light of inquiry (*Vichāra*) begin to dawn.

Shankara's Interpretation: The Dawn of Mumukshutva

In his *Bhagavad Gita Bhāṣya*, **Adi Shankaracharya** treats Arjuna's sorrow not as a moral failure but as a *turning point* — the **birth of spiritual aspiration (Mumukshutva)**.

He explains that Arjuna's despondency is the sign of a maturing soul. The warrior's refusal to act blindly, his refusal to accept tradition without discernment, marks the awakening of true intelligence (*Viveka*). The pain of conflict, in this sense, becomes a **spiritual catalyst**.

Shankara writes that suffering (*duḥkha*) can be the doorway to knowledge if it compels introspection. When external solutions fail, the seeker turns inward. Thus, *Vishāda* — despair — becomes *Yoga* — the discipline that unites the finite with the infinite.

Despair as a Path to Illumination

In Shankara's vision, Arjuna's sorrow is sacred because it strips away illusion. Until this moment, Arjuna identified with his role as warrior, brother, and prince. But when these identities collide, their impermanence is exposed.

Through this breakdown of self-concepts, the deeper question arises: *Who am I?* — the very inquiry (*Ātma Vichāra*) that leads to liberation.

The first chapter, therefore, is not merely a prelude to divine teaching but a spiritual mirror. It shows that the human journey begins not in perfection but in **perplexity**. The heart must first experience fragmentation before it can seek unity.

Philosophical Insight: The Nature of Human Suffering

According to Shankara's Advaita Vedānta, all suffering stems from **misidentification** — the confusion between the Self (*Ātman*), which is eternal and unchanging, and the body-mind complex, which is transient.

Arjuna's grief arises because he sees himself as the *doer* and *enjoyer*, entangled in relations and outcomes. His despair, therefore, is the symptom of **ignorance (Avidyā)** — the same ignorance that binds every human being to the cycle of birth and death (*Saṃsāra*).

Yet, paradoxically, this ignorance also gives rise to inquiry. When pain pierces illusion, the longing for truth is born. Thus, what appears as darkness is, in truth, the **first light of wisdom**.

Shankara's Psychological Reading

Long before modern psychology, Shankara perceived the stages of the human mind's evolution toward truth.

1. **Delusion (Moha)** – Identification with the non-self.
2. **Despair (Vishāda)** – Recognition of contradiction within worldly attachments.
3. **Inquiry (Vichāra)** – The turn inward, seeking a higher resolution.
4. **Understanding (Bodha)** – Knowledge of one's true Self as pure consciousness.

Arjuna stands at the second stage — despair. Krishna's teachings in the subsequent chapters will guide him toward inquiry and understanding.

Shankara's compassion lies in his refusal to condemn Arjuna's breakdown; instead, he honors it as the **beginning of Yoga**. True spirituality does not deny confusion — it transforms it.

Spiritual Symbolism of the Battlefield

In the Advaitic lens, Kurukshetra represents **life itself** — the inevitable field of choices and consequences. The armies symbolize conflicting forces within consciousness: attachment versus detachment, ignorance versus wisdom, ego versus Self.

The *Gita* begins where action seems impossible, for only then can Krishna — the divine teacher, the voice of the Self — begin to speak. The Lord's silence before Arjuna's despair signifies that divine wisdom does not arise until the human mind exhausts its self-created certainties.

Reflections for the Seeker

1. **Suffering as a Sacred Threshold**
   When life brings inner conflict, see it not as punishment but as an invitation. The discomfort that disturbs the ego awakens the seeker.
2. **Courage to Question**
   Like Arjuna, have the courage to pause and question before acting blindly. Doubt, when sincere, is a form of devotion — it opens the door to understanding.
3. **Transforming Despair into Discipline**
   The mind's restlessness can be turned into focus when directed toward inquiry. Every confusion, if examined deeply, can lead to clarity.
4. **The Inner Battlefield**
   Recognize your own Kurukshetra — the space where

worldly attachments and spiritual insight struggle for dominance. In that awareness, transformation begins.

Conclusion: The Beginning of the Journey

Arjuna's despondency marks the true commencement of the *Bhagavad Gita*. It is the **moment of surrender** — not to defeat, but to truth. Through the eyes of Adi Shankaracharya, we see that Yoga begins not with achievement but with humility, not with certainty but with the honest recognition of confusion.

In the silence that follows Arjuna's tears, the eternal dialogue between the human and the divine begins.

"To know that one does not know — that is the beginning of wisdom."

— *Adi Shankaracharya, Vivekachudamani*

The Yoga of Knowledge

The wise grieve neither for the living nor for the dead. Never was there a time when I was not, nor you, nor these kings; nor will any of us cease to be hereafter.
— *Bhagavad Gita* 2.11–12

The Turning Point of the Dialogue

The second chapter of the *Bhagavad Gita* marks the turning of the tide — from despair to discernment, from emotion to inquiry. Arjuna's surrender in the previous chapter opens the space for **Śrī Krishna's teaching**, and the Lord's first instruction is not consolation but **clarity**.

Krishna begins not by promising victory or comfort, but by pointing toward truth: the **Self (Ātman)** is eternal, untouched by birth or death. This revelation transforms the nature of the discourse from moral struggle to metaphysical vision.

For **Adi Shankaracharya**, this chapter is the *heart of the Gita*. It contains the seed of the entire Advaitic philosophy — that liberation arises not through action or devotion alone but through **true knowledge** of one's Self as Brahman.

Shankara's Interpretation: Knowledge as the Supreme Yoga

In his *Bhāṣya*, Shankara interprets Krishna's opening words as a **direct refutation of ignorance (Avidyā)** — the root of all grief. Arjuna's sorrow stemmed from identifying himself with the perishable body and regarding others as separate beings. Krishna dissolves this delusion with the light of **Sāṅkhya**, the discriminative knowledge that reveals the difference between the eternal and the transient.

For Shankara, *Sāṅkhya* here does not mean the dualistic system of Kapila but rather **the knowledge of Reality** — the insight that the Self is pure consciousness, beyond body, mind, and emotion. The body may perish, but the Self is unborn, undying, and unchanging.

Thus begins the first true instruction of the *Gita*:

To know oneself as the eternal witness is to be free from sorrow.

The Doctrine of the Eternal Self

Shankara emphasizes that Krishna's teaching on the immortality of the Self is not metaphoric or poetic; it is ontological truth.

"Weapons cannot cut it, fire cannot burn it, water cannot wet it, wind cannot dry it."
— *Bhagavad Gita* 2.23

These verses, Shankara explains, describe the **immutable nature of the Self** — beyond material causation, impervious to change.

Ignorance alone creates the illusion of individuality. The body acts, the mind feels, but the witnessing consciousness remains unchanged — like the sun reflecting on many waters, appearing as many yet remaining one.

The realization of this truth — that *Ātman is Brahman* — is the beginning of liberation (*Moksha*).

The Nature of Action and Duty

Having established the reality of the Self, Krishna turns to action (*Karma*). If the Self is eternal and untouched, why act at all?

Shankara resolves this apparent contradiction with subtle insight:
Actions belong to the body and mind, not to the Self. The wise person acts **without attachment**, performing duty as a means of purifying the intellect (*Antaḥkaraṇa Śuddhi*).

Thus, action is not renounced but **transformed** — no longer driven by ego or desire, but by harmony with the cosmic order (*Dharma*).

This is the birth of **Karma Yoga** within the framework of **Jnana Yoga**. For Shankara, Karma does not lead directly to liberation, but it refines the mind to receive knowledge. As a lamp must be steady to reflect light, the intellect must be pure to reflect truth.

The Equanimity of the Wise

A pivotal teaching in this chapter is Krishna's call for **equanimity**:

"Be alike in success and failure; such evenness is called Yoga."
— *Bhagavad Gita* 2.48

Shankara explains that equanimity (*Samatva*) arises naturally from the knowledge of the Self. When one no longer identifies with outcomes, likes, or dislikes, all actions become spontaneous expressions of wisdom.

Such a person is not indifferent but serene — engaged in the world without being entangled by it.

In Shankara's words, *Yoga* is the "steadiness of mind in the midst of opposites." It is the state in which the intellect, free from agitation, reflects the truth of Brahman as a still lake reflects the moon.

The Stages of Inner Transformation

Shankara outlines a progression of inner growth through this chapter:

1. **Confusion (Moha)** – Arjuna's initial state of despair.
2. **Instruction (Upadeśa)** – Krishna's teaching on the Self.
3. **Discrimination (Viveka)** – Understanding the eternal and the transient.
4. **Detachment (Vairāgya)** – Freedom from desire and fear.
5. **Stability (Samatva)** – Equanimity in pleasure and pain.
6. **Knowledge (Jnana)** – Direct realization of Self as Brahman.

The chapter closes with the image of the **Sthita-Prajña** — the "one of steady wisdom." This ideal, Shankara explains, is not a remote ascetic but a person who lives in the world without being bound by it.

The Sthita-Prajña: Portrait of the Liberated Mind

"When a man gives up all desires of the heart and is satisfied in the Self by the Self, he is said to be of steady wisdom."
— *Bhagavad Gita* 2.55

For Shankara, this is the culmination of Yoga. The Sthita-Prajña lives with total awareness, not suppressing emotion but seeing through its illusion. Desires may arise, but they no longer possess. Fear may visit, but it no longer controls.

He neither rejoices in gain nor laments in loss. He walks the earth as one awake among dreamers — inwardly free, outwardly serene.

Shankara describes this state as **Jivanmukti** — liberation while living. Such a being is not indifferent to the world but is rooted in an unbroken awareness of Brahman, from which compassion naturally flows.

Philosophical Summary: The Yoga of Knowledge

In Shankara's Advaitic reading, this chapter contains the essence of the entire Gita:

- The **Self (Ātman)** is eternal and indivisible.
- **Ignorance (Avidyā)** alone causes suffering.
- **Knowledge (Jnana)** alone brings liberation.
- **Action (Karma)** serves as a preparatory discipline.
- **Equanimity (Samatva)** is the expression of realized wisdom.

Thus, *Sāṅkhya Yoga* is not mere philosophy but **the awakening of right vision** — seeing the Self as the Self, untainted by the transient play of names and forms.

Reflections for the Seeker

1. **Know the Eternal Within**
   The body changes, thoughts come and go, but awareness remains unchanged. Dwell in that awareness — it is your true Self.
2. **Act Without Attachment**
   Perform duties as offerings, not as transactions. Freedom lies in action done without expectation.
3. **Cultivate Equanimity**
   Success and failure, pleasure and pain — all are waves on the same ocean of consciousness. Watch them rise and fall without losing your stillness.
4. **Contemplate the Witness**
   Observe the mind as it moves, but remember: you

are not the movement, you are the observer. In this recognition lies peace.

Conclusion: Knowledge as Liberation

In the **Sāṅkhya Yoga**, Shankara reveals that true freedom begins with right understanding. The battle of Kurukshetra continues, but its meaning changes. Arjuna is no longer the fearful warrior — he becomes the seeker of truth.

This chapter transforms grief into vision, action into worship, and knowledge into liberation. As Shankara reminds us, when ignorance ends, nothing new is gained — only the eternal Self is seen as it always was.

"When the sun rises, the darkness does not go anywhere — it simply ceases to appear."
— Adi Shankaracharya

The Path of Selfless Action

Action is superior to inaction. Even the maintenance of your body would be impossible without action.
— *Bhagavad Gita* 3.8

From Knowledge to Action

Having established in *Sāṅkhya Yoga* that knowledge of the Self is the ultimate liberating force, Krishna now turns to the practical question that often troubles seekers: *If knowledge alone leads to liberation, why act at all?*

Arjuna's confusion echoes a timeless dilemma — should the seeker withdraw from worldly duties in pursuit of wisdom, or act amidst the world while remaining unattached?

Adi Shankaracharya's interpretation illuminates this question with characteristic precision. He asserts that action (*Karma*) does not in itself liberate the soul, yet it plays a vital role in preparing the mind for liberation. Like the preliminary cleansing before the mirror reveals its reflection, **selfless action purifies the intellect**, enabling the light of knowledge to dawn.

Shankara's Perspective: Karma as a Purifier, Not a Deliverer

In his *Bhāṣya* on this chapter, Shankara describes *Karma Yoga* as a **disciplinary stage** on the spiritual journey. For the unprepared mind — restless, distracted, or ego-centered — the direct pursuit of knowledge is difficult.

Therefore, action performed with detachment and offered to the Divine (*Īśvara Arpaṇa Buddhi*) becomes a form of spiritual practice. Through selfless service, the mind is cleansed of *Rāga* (attachment) and *Dveṣa* (aversion).

"Action done without desire for fruit purifies the mind;
when purity of mind is gained, knowledge arises spontaneously."

— *Shankara, Gita Bhāṣya 3.3*

Shankara insists that once true knowledge arises, action as a means ceases — yet the realized sage may still act out of compassion, for the welfare of the world (*Lokasaṅgraha*).

The Law of Action

Krishna declares that all beings are bound to act according to their nature. Even in inaction, there is movement — breathing, thinking, living. Shankara interprets this as an illustration of the **inescapability of Prakṛti** (nature).

He teaches that the wise act in harmony with this natural order, **without egoic ownership**. The deluded, however, imagine "I am the doer," and thereby bind themselves to the consequences of their deeds.

Shankara's Advaitic vision replaces this false doership with **witness-consciousness** (*Sākṣitva*). The Self neither acts nor causes action; it merely illumines. Actions unfold in the field of nature, while the Self remains the eternal witness.

Renunciation Through Understanding

"He who sees inaction in action, and action in inaction,
he is the wise one among men."

— *Bhagavad Gita* 4.18

Though this verse belongs to the next chapter, Shankara refers to its principle here: **true renunciation is mental, not physical**. To renounce the sense of doership is far greater than abandoning work itself.

Thus, the householder who acts selflessly may be nearer to liberation than the ascetic who withdraws but still clings to identity.

Shankara redefines spirituality not as escape from the world, but **seeing the world rightly** — as the play of Prakṛti upon the unchanging Self.

Karma and Dharma

Shankara affirms Krishna's call to perform one's **Svadharma** — one's natural and social duty — without attachment. This concept, often misunderstood, does not imply mechanical obedience to role or tradition.

Rather, *Svadharma* represents alignment with one's **innate disposition** and spiritual maturity. For Arjuna, as a warrior, avoiding battle would mean violating his nature and stagnating his evolution.

In Shankara's eyes, evasion of duty from attachment to comfort or aversion to conflict only strengthens ignorance. Performing one's dharma selflessly, however, refines the mind, loosens the ego, and prepares it for knowledge.

The Psychology of Karma Yoga

Shankara subtly bridges **ethics and enlightenment**. He shows that selfless action reorients the psyche from self-centered striving to selfless awareness.

The key psychological transformations are:

1. **From Desire to Devotion** – Acting not for gain, but as offering to the Divine.
2. **From Ego to Instrumentality** – Seeing oneself as a medium of the cosmic order.

3. **From Anxiety to Equanimity** – Accepting outcomes with serenity, knowing that results are governed by universal law, not personal will.

This transformation does not suppress action but **transfigures it**. The hands continue their work, but the heart rests in freedom.

The Wise and the Ignorant

Krishna explains that the wise act without bondage, yet the ignorant imitate action with attachment. Therefore, the enlightened sage continues to act — not for personal gain, but to guide others.

Shankara notes that **compassion** motivates the actions of the liberated. Though they have nothing to gain, their presence sustains the moral and spiritual rhythm of the world. Their work becomes a form of teaching — silent, effortless, and luminous.

In contrast, actions driven by ego lead to fatigue, pride, and rebirth. The ignorant, believing "I act," are caught in the web of results.

Action as Worship

Shankara interprets Krishna's declaration — *"Yajñārthāt karmaṇo'nyatra loko'ya� karma-bandhanaḥ"* — "The world is bound by action unless it is done as sacrifice."

Here, *Yajña* (sacrifice) is not a ritual but a **spiritual attitude** — the recognition that all actions belong to the whole, not to the individual.

When the mind acts in this spirit of surrender, every duty becomes worship, every breath becomes prayer. Action then ceases to create bondage; it becomes **a movement of the Divine through the individual**.

Philosophical Summary: The Path of Selfless Action

According to Shankara's Advaitic insight, *Karma Yoga* holds a unique place in the seeker's progression:

- **Purpose:** Purification of mind (*Antaḥkaraṇa Śuddhi*).
- **Process:** Selfless action without desire for fruit.
- **Outcome:** Readiness for knowledge (*Adhikāritva*).
- **Culmination:** Renunciation of doership in the light of Self-realization.

Thus, *Karma Yoga* is both the **discipline of purification** and the **foundation of liberation**. Action, when freed from attachment, becomes meditation in motion.

Reflections for the Seeker

1. **Act, but Surrender the Result**
   Let every deed be an offering. What you cannot control, release; what you can, perform with love and precision.
2. **Transform Work into Worship**
   Whether in profession, service, or daily duty, act as if the Divine works through you. The joy of work is born when the ego steps aside.
3. **Renounce the Doer, Not the Deed**
   Renunciation is an inner state. Continue to fulfill your responsibilities, but without claiming ownership.
4. **Purify the Mind Through Service**
   Selfless service cleanses the mirror of consciousness. Every act done for the welfare of others refines the Self's reflection.

Conclusion: Work as the Way to Stillness

For **Adi Shankaracharya**, *Karma Yoga* is not a contradiction to knowledge — it is its preparation.
The journey from *Vishāda* (despair) to *Sāṅkhya* (knowledge) finds its living expression in *Karma* (selfless action).

Through right understanding, work becomes meditation, and daily life becomes the crucible in which ignorance is burned away.

In the silence that follows selfless action, the mind becomes still — and in that stillness, the truth of Brahman shines forth.

"Let action burn the impurities of mind,
and knowledge illumine what remains — the Self, eternal and pure."
— *Adi Shankaracharya*

Union Through Knowledge and Renunciation

As the blazing fire reduces fuel to ashes,
so does the fire of knowledge burn all actions to ashes.
— *Bhagavad Gita* 4.37

The Dawn of Spiritual Clarity

With Arjuna's understanding of action refined through *Karma Yoga*, the dialogue now ascends toward its philosophical summit. The fourth chapter unveils the **divine mystery of knowledge and renunciation**, showing how wisdom transcends even righteous action.

Krishna reveals the sacred lineage of this eternal Yoga — first taught to the Sun-god Vivasvān, then to Manu, then to the royal sages, and finally to Arjuna.

This lineage, according to **Adi Shankaracharya**, signifies that truth is timeless. Knowledge of the Self (*Ātma-Jñāna*) is not new; it is the rediscovery of what has always been known by awakened beings.

Shankara explains that *Jñāna Karma Sannyāsa Yoga* is the confluence where **knowledge dissolves action**, where understanding transforms the very fabric of duty into liberation.

Shankara's Interpretation: Knowledge as the Final Purifier

In his *Bhāṣya*, Shankara emphasizes that all scriptural paths — ritual, devotion, meditation, and service — find fulfillment in **knowledge of the Self**.

Action (*Karma*), when performed without desire, prepares the mind; but knowledge alone **destroys ignorance**, which is the root of bondage.

When ignorance ends, there remains no doer, no deed, and no result — only the infinite Brahman, self-luminous and free.

"All actions, whether virtuous or sinful, vanish as water on a lotus leaf,
when the Self is known as non-doer."
— *Shankara, Gita Bhāṣya 4.18*

Thus, the fire of knowledge (*Jñānāgni*) consumes the accumulated tendencies of action (*Karma-saṃskāra*), leaving only the clarity of awareness.

The Divine Incarnation: A Manifestation of Compassion

This chapter also unveils one of the most beloved verses of the *Gita*:

"Whenever righteousness declines and unrighteousness prevails,
I manifest Myself."
— *Bhagavad Gita* 4.7

Shankara offers a subtle interpretation of this verse. For him, **the incarnation of the Divine (Avatāra)** is not the descent of a separate deity, but the **manifestation of Brahman** in human form for the guidance of seekers.

The Infinite, though untouched and changeless, appears as form — just as space seems to take shape within a vessel.
Krishna's descent is, therefore, **a compassionate illusion born of divine will**, not a transformation of the Absolute.

The purpose of this manifestation, Shankara writes, is *Lokasaṅgraha* — the preservation of cosmic harmony and the restoration of Dharma. Through the Avatāra, the timeless wisdom of Brahman becomes accessible to finite minds.

The Synthesis of Knowledge and Action

A key theme in this chapter is the reconciliation of **knowledge and renunciation**. Arjuna fears that knowledge might lead to passivity; Shankara clarifies that this is a misunderstanding.

Action, when performed by the ignorant, binds.
Action, when performed by the wise, **purifies**.
But in the enlightened, there is no sense of *"I act."*

In the realized being, action and renunciation coexist effortlessly — just as a flower gives fragrance without intent.
Such a person acts for the welfare of the world, yet inwardly abides in stillness.

Shankara declares that this is the **highest state of Yoga** — the fusion of *Karma* and *Jñāna*, where life itself becomes meditation.

The Fourfold Division of Works

Krishna explains that actions are of four kinds —

1. **Nitya Karma** – obligatory duties (like daily worship),
2. **Naimittika Karma** – occasional duties (like rituals),
3. **Kāmya Karma** – desire-driven actions, and
4. **Niṣiddha Karma** – prohibited actions.

Shankara clarifies that only the first two, performed without attachment, aid spiritual evolution. The latter two bind the soul through desire and ignorance.

When the seeker rises to knowledge, even the obligatory duties fall away, for the doer himself dissolves.

This is **Sannyāsa** — not a physical renunciation but a mental transcendence of all roles and results.

The Central Image: The Fire of Wisdom

The *Gita* compares wisdom to fire.
Shankara elaborates that **fire is both purifier and destroyer** — it consumes impurities and reveals what is pure. Similarly, the fire of Self-knowledge burns away ignorance and reveals Brahman, which was never absent.

The ignorant see fire as external; the wise recognize it within — as consciousness itself.

Thus, the chapter's imagery is inwardly alchemical: knowledge is the fire, ignorance the fuel, and realization the flame that consumes both.

Faith and Discernment

"The ignorant, the faithless, and the doubting soul perish. The one who has faith, who is devoted and disciplined, attains knowledge."
— *Bhagavad Gita* 4.40

Shankara interprets *Śraddhā* (faith) not as blind belief but as **intuitive conviction born of purity**.
Faith is the mind's openness to truth; without it, knowledge cannot settle.
Doubt (*Saṃśaya*) clouds understanding, while sincerity clears the path to realization.

Faith, discipline, and discernment together form the **threefold foundation** of spiritual growth — leading the aspirant from practice to perception.

Philosophical Summary: Jñāna Karma Sannyāsa Yoga

Shankara's Advaitic synthesis of this chapter can be summarized thus:

- **Action (Karma)** is the means to purification, not liberation.
- **Knowledge (Jñāna)** is the direct destroyer of ignorance.
- **Renunciation (Sannyāsa)** is mental non-attachment, not withdrawal.
- **Divine Incarnation (Avatāra)** is Brahman's compassionate expression in time.
- **Faith (Śraddhā)** and **discipline (Tapas)** stabilize knowledge.

The culmination of all action is renunciation, and the culmination of all renunciation is knowledge — this is the spiritual parabola of the *Gita* as seen by Shankara.

Reflections for the Seeker

1. **Let Knowledge Purify Your Actions**
   Work as worship, but remember: the ultimate offering is ignorance itself. Let every act be kindled by awareness.
2. **Seek Inner Renunciation**
   True Sannyāsa is freedom from the thought "I act." You may live amidst movement yet remain unmoved within.
3. **Recognize the Divine in All Forms**
   The Avatāra is not history alone — it is the presence of wisdom manifesting wherever Dharma is restored, even within one's own heart.
4. **Trust the Fire Within**
   Knowledge may arise slowly, but once lit, it never dies. Feed that inner flame with sincerity, reflection, and love for truth.

Conclusion: The Alchemy of Knowledge

Through Shankara's eyes, *Jñāna Karma Sannyāsa Yoga* is the **alchemy of the soul**.

It transforms the seeker's relationship with the world — from striving to surrender, from doing to being.

In the fire of awareness, all actions lose their binding power, and what remains is stillness — luminous, eternal, and free.

"When ignorance burns in the fire of wisdom,
the ashes that remain are peace."
— *Adi Shankaracharya*

The Renunciation of Action

He who neither hates nor desires should be known as a true renouncer;
free from the pairs of opposites, O mighty-armed, he is easily set free from bondage.
— *Bhagavad Gita* 5.3

The Question of Renunciation

The human mind, upon hearing that liberation is attained through knowledge, often assumes that **renunciation** — the giving up of all action — is the highest path. Arjuna too is caught in this tension: should he act as a warrior, or renounce action in pursuit of peace?

In this chapter, Krishna and **Adi Shankaracharya's commentary** together reveal that *true renunciation* (*Sannyāsa*) is **not the abandonment of action**, but the abandonment of **egoic ownership**.

Shankara dismantles the misconception that freedom lies in withdrawal. Rather, he shows that **freedom is an inner condition** — the state in which the mind remains untouched by the movements of life, just as a lotus leaf remains dry though it rests on water.

Shankara's Interpretation: Inward Renunciation

In his *Bhāṣya*, Shankara draws a crucial distinction between **Karma Sannyāsa** (outer renunciation) and **Karma Yoga** (action in renunciation). He affirms that for those whose minds are purified through knowledge, even while engaged in action, there is no bondage.

"He who knows himself as non-doer, though acting, truly does not act."

— *Shankara, Gita Bhāṣya 5.7*

Thus, Shankara identifies two paths that ultimately merge into one:

1. The path of **Action without Attachment (Karma Yoga)** — for those still purifying the mind.
2. The path of **Renunciation through Knowledge (Jñāna Sannyāsa)** — for those whose understanding is mature.

While outwardly different, both converge in the realization of non-doership (*Akartṛtva*).

Equality of Paths

Krishna declares that both action and renunciation, when performed with wisdom, lead to the same goal. Yet, of the two, **Karma Yoga is superior**, because it is more accessible and natural for most seekers.

Shankara clarifies that complete renunciation — the total withdrawal from action — requires deep knowledge and detachment. For others, forced inactivity can strengthen the ego and create inner conflict.

Action done without attachment, however, gradually ripens into wisdom. Thus, Karma Yoga becomes the **bridge to Sannyāsa**, and Sannyāsa becomes the **flowering of Karma Yoga**.

The True Sannyāsin

Who, then, is a true renouncer?

Shankara answers:

It is not the one who abandons duties, but the one who **abandons identification** with the doer and the enjoyer.

"He who is without hatred or desire,
who has mastered the pairs of opposites,
is easily liberated from bondage."
— *Bhagavad Gita* 5.3

The genuine Sannyāsin may walk in the marketplace or dwell in the forest — it matters not. His mind rests in Brahman. He acts spontaneously, without self-reference, without motive. His renunciation is **inner, not external**.

The Stillness Within Action

Krishna teaches that the sage perceives action in inaction, and inaction in action — a paradox that Shankara explains with penetrating simplicity.

When the body acts but the mind is free from the notion "I act," that is **inaction within action**.

When the mind is still but the ego remains, that is **action within inaction**.

Shankara shows that liberation is not achieved through what one does or avoids, but through **seeing rightly**.

When the false identification with the body and mind ceases, all actions lose their binding power.

The sage acts, yet is as if he acts not. He renounces, yet nothing is left to renounce.

The Self as Witness

Shankara reiterates that all actions arise from **Prakṛti** — the play of the three *Guṇas* (modes of nature): *Sattva* (purity), *Rajas* (activity), and *Tamas* (inertia).

The Self (*Ātman*), being pure consciousness, merely **witnesses** these movements.

"The wise, knowing that the Self acts not,
though seeing, hearing, touching, smelling, eating, walking, sleeping, breathing,
remain untainted."
— *Bhagavad Gita* 5.8–9

Shankara's insight here is profound: liberation is not an act of becoming something new — it is the recognition that one was never bound. The realization of the Self as non-doer dissolves the illusion of Karma itself.

The Vision of the Universal Self

A striking element of this chapter is Krishna's call to equality of vision:

"The wise see the same Self in a learned priest, a cow, an elephant, a dog, and even an outcast."
— *Bhagavad Gita* 5.18

For Shankara, this verse embodies the essence of **Advaita Vedānta**. The enlightened one perceives no difference in essence between beings — only variation in forms. The multiplicity of appearances hides a single consciousness.

This is the state of **Samadarśitva** — equal vision — where love and compassion arise spontaneously, not as moral duty but as natural expression of unity.

Inner Freedom and Bliss

The renouncer established in the Self experiences an inward joy beyond sense contact.

"Having found that happiness which is beyond the senses,
he is not shaken even by great sorrow."
— *Bhagavad Gita* 5.21

Shankara interprets this happiness as **Ānanda**, the bliss of the Self. It is not emotional excitement but **existential completeness** — the peace that arises when the seeking mind dissolves into pure being.

Such joy is not created; it is revealed when ignorance subsides.
Just as the sun shines constantly, but clouds veil it, so the bliss of the Self is constant, hidden only by desire and delusion.

Philosophical Summary: Karma Sannyāsa Yoga

According to Shankara's Advaitic interpretation:

- **Renunciation** is the giving up of ego, not of activity.
- **Action and renunciation** are complementary stages of one process.
- **Liberation** arises from knowledge, not from physical withdrawal.
- **Equality of vision** reveals Brahman in all beings.
- **Inner joy** is the fragrance of freedom, not the result of external achievement.

Thus, *Karma Sannyāsa Yoga* represents the **mature stage of Yoga**, where action ceases to bind and knowledge blossoms naturally within life itself.

Reflections for the Seeker

1. **Renounce the Ego, Not the World**
   Live, act, and serve, but remember that the doer is only an appearance in consciousness.
2. **Find Stillness in Motion**
   Let your actions flow like a river — purposeful yet unattached. Stillness is not the absence of movement, but the absence of resistance.
3. **See the One in All**
   The truest renunciation is compassion — seeing no "other." Unity dissolves judgment and breeds peace.
4. **Abide in Inner Joy**
   Happiness that depends on outcome is fragile. Dis-

cover the joy that arises from being itself — the joy of pure awareness.

Conclusion: Renunciation as Freedom

For **Adi Shankaracharya**, the essence of *Karma Sannyāsa Yoga* is **freedom within action**.

The outer life may continue with its rhythms, but the inner life abides in silence.

When knowledge dawns, renunciation is no longer practiced — it becomes one's natural state.

The wise act without motive, speak without claim, and rest without fear.

In the perfect equilibrium of knowing and doing, the soul finds peace that no circumstance can disturb.

"Renunciation is not of the world, but of the thought of 'mine.'

When that thought ends, the Self alone remains."

— *Adi Shankaracharya*

The Yoga of Meditation

Let a man lift himself by himself;
let him not degrade himself.
For the Self alone is the friend of the Self,
and the Self alone is the enemy of the Self.
— *Bhagavad Gita 6.5*

The Stillness After Understanding

Having guided Arjuna from despair (*Vishāda*) through knowledge (*Sāṅkhya*) and selfless action (*Karma Yoga*), Krishna now leads him toward the practice that stabilizes wisdom — **meditation**, or *Dhyāna Yoga*.

For **Adi Shankaracharya**, this chapter is the *bridge* between knowledge and realization.

Right understanding, he explains, ripens into liberation only when the mind becomes steady — when thoughts, purified by Karma Yoga and illuminated by knowledge, are dissolved in the contemplation of the Self.

Meditation, therefore, is not another method to *reach* Brahman, but the means by which the restless intellect is made transparent enough to **recognize** Brahman as ever-present.

Shankara's View: Meditation as Abidance in the Self

In his *Bhāṣya*, Shankara describes *Dhyāna* as **single-pointed absorption** (*Ekāgratā*) in the truth "I am Brahman." The seeker withdraws the senses from external objects and directs awareness inward. The mind, no longer scattered among desires, rests in its source like a flame undisturbed by wind.

This is the stage of **steady abidance (Nididhyāsana)** — the lived realization of what has already been intellectually understood.

"Meditation is not thinking of Brahman, but being Brahman knowingly."
— *Shankara, Gita Bhāṣya 6.19*

The Discipline of Mind

Krishna teaches that the mind can be both a friend and an enemy.
When ruled by desire, it binds; when governed by discernment, it liberates.

Shankara elaborates: the mind must be trained with compassion, not violence. Control is not suppression, but **re-education** — returning it again and again to awareness.

The tools are:

- **Abhyāsa** – repeated practice of recollecting the Self,
- **Vairāgya** – dispassion toward fleeting objects, and
- **Śama** – quietude born of understanding.

Through these, the scattered energies of thought gather into the still point of meditation.

Solitude and Inner Space

"In a clean, secluded place, let the yogi sit upon a firm seat, neither too high nor too low, with the mind subdued and the senses controlled."
— *Bhagavad Gita 6.11–12*

Shankara interprets this not merely as physical instruction but as **symbolic guidance**.
The "clean place" represents a pure mind free from agitation.
The "firm seat" is the stable understanding that one is not the body.
"Solitude" is the withdrawal from dependency on external validation.

The true hermitage, Shankara reminds, is within one's own heart.

Equality in Meditation

Krishna describes the yogi who has conquered the mind as one who sees joy and sorrow, gain and loss, honor and dishonor alike.

Shankara comments that such equality arises naturally when the mind abides in Brahman.
The opposites belong to the field of experience, but the Self is untouched by them — like the sky unstained by passing clouds.

When equanimity becomes effortless, meditation ceases to be a practice and becomes a **state of being**.

The Challenge of Restlessness

Arjuna confesses:

"The mind is restless, turbulent, powerful, and obstinate.
I think it is as hard to control as the wind."
— *Bhagavad Gita 6.34*

Shankara agrees — control of mind is indeed the greatest challenge. Yet he assures that **discipline and detachment** make it possible.

The mind's turbulence arises from long-standing habits (*Vāsanās*). Each act of awareness weakens these tendencies. Gradually, the seeker experiences longer intervals of silence, until silence itself becomes the natural background of consciousness.

The Yogi and the World

For Shankara, meditation does not require escape from life. The realized yogi lives amid activity, yet his mind is anchored in stillness. He may walk, teach, or serve, but inwardly he is free — watching all movements as waves on the ocean of Self.

"He who sees the Self in all beings and all beings in the Self, such a one, though engaged in action, never separates from Me."
— *Bhagavad Gita 6.29*

This verse, Shankara says, describes **the culmination of meditation** — vision without division.

The Fate of the Unfulfilled Seeker

Arjuna fears that the practitioner who fails to perfect meditation may lose both worldly and spiritual gain.
Krishna consoles him that sincere effort is never wasted.

Shankara elaborates: the impressions of meditation persist across lifetimes, reawakening as spiritual inclination. The soul, propelled by its purity, resumes its journey until realization is attained.

Thus, no genuine effort toward truth ever perishes.

The Supreme Yogi

The chapter concludes with Krishna's declaration:

"Among all yogis, he who worships Me with faith and whose inner Self is united with Me,
I hold to be the most steadfast."
— *Bhagavad Gita 6.47*

Shankara interprets "worship" here not as ritual, but as **abidance in knowledge** — the unwavering recognition of the Self as Brahman.
Such a yogi has transcended both practice and practitioner; he lives as awareness itself.

Philosophical Summary: Dhyāna Yoga

According to Shankara's Advaitic exposition:

- Meditation (*Dhyāna*) is continuous remembrance of the Self, not mental activity.
- Control of mind is achieved through practice (*Abhyāsa*) and detachment (*Vairāgya*).
- Solitude and purity symbolize inner independence from sense objects.
- The culmination of meditation is **identity with Brahman** — where subject and object dissolve.

Meditation, therefore, is not an act but **the cessation of all acts** — the resting of awareness in itself.

Reflections for the Seeker

1. **Cultivate Gentle Discipline**
   Guide the mind like a child — firmly yet kindly — back to awareness.
2. **Create Inner Solitude**
   Withdraw daily into silence; even amid others, dwell inwardly alone in peace.
3. **Witness Without Interference**
   Observe thoughts without struggle. The watcher and the watched are one consciousness.
4. **Rest in Faith**
   Progress in meditation is subtle. Trust the process; sincerity itself is success.

Conclusion: Meditation as Abiding in Oneness

In **Shankara's vision**, *Dhyāna Yoga* is the flowering of all previous disciplines.
Knowledge reveals truth; meditation **stabilizes** it.
When the mind is dissolved in the stillness of Brahman, duality ends.

The yogi no longer meditates *on* the Self — he **is** the Self. Action and inaction, inside and outside, all merge into one expanse of awareness.

"When the mind becomes silent,
Brahman shines as one's own Self —
not as an object known,
but as the knower alone."
— *Adi Shankaracharya*

Knowledge and Wisdom

Hear now, O Arjuna, how, with your mind attached to Me and taking refuge in Me,
you shall know Me fully—without any remainder of doubt.
— *Bhagavad Gita 7.1*

From Concept to Realization

The journey through the *Gita* now crosses a vital threshold. After meditation's stillness, Krishna introduces the seeker to the **essence of divine knowledge (Jñāna)** and its direct realization (**Vijñāna**).

For **Ādi Shankaracharya**, this chapter unveils the transition from intellectual comprehension to **living wisdom**—from knowing *about* Brahman to *abiding as* Brahman. Knowledge (*Jñāna*) is like seeing the ocean on a map; realization (*Vijñāna*) is standing on its shore and feeling its vastness.

This is the yoga of **illumined understanding**—where the knower, the known, and knowledge dissolve into one awareness.

Shankara's Vision: The Twofold Knowledge

Shankara begins his commentary by distinguishing two kinds of knowledge:

1. **Lower Knowledge (Apara Vidya):** comprehension of the phenomenal—rituals, scriptures, and intellectual study; and
2. **Higher Knowledge (Para Vidya):** the direct intuition of Brahman, beyond thought and word.

Krishna's "knowledge and wisdom" refer to these two levels. The lower purifies and prepares; the higher liberates. When both unite, life becomes a reflection of truth.

"Knowing Brahman as one's own Self is Jñāna;
remaining established in that truth is Vijñāna."
— *Shankara, Gita Bhāṣya 7.2*

The Twofold Nature of Reality

Krishna reveals:

"Earth, water, fire, air, ether, mind, intellect, and ego—these constitute My eightfold nature.
Beyond this, know My higher nature, which is the life-principle sustaining the world."
— *Bhagavad Gita 7.4-5*

Shankara interprets these verses through the lens of **Advaita**: the first eight represent **Prakṛti**, the material and psychological manifestation; the "higher nature" is **Puruṣa**, the conscious principle—the *Ātman* that enlivens all forms.

The universe thus has two aspects: the seen (mutable) and the seer (immutable). Mistaking the seen for the seer is ignorance; recognizing their unity is wisdom.

The One in the Many

Krishna declares Himself the essence behind every phenomenon—the taste in water, the light in the moon and sun, the sacred syllable *Om* in the Vedas.

Shankara explains that these are **illustrations of immanence**. Brahman pervades everything as the substratum of all experience. Just as gold underlies all ornaments, consciousness underlies all names and forms.

The enlightened vision, therefore, does not reject the world but **sees through it**—seeing only Brahman, appearing as all.

The Veil of Māyā

"By My divine illusion (*Māyā*), I am not manifest to all.
The deluded world knows Me not as unborn and imperishable."
— *Bhagavad Gita 7.25*

Shankara elucidates *Māyā* as the mysterious power that causes the One to appear as many. It is not an independent reality but the **veil of ignorance** that obscures the truth of unity.

The world seems dualistic because of this projection. Once knowledge dawns, the illusion fades, and the eternal witness—pure consciousness—shines self-luminous.

Māyā does not need to be destroyed; it simply needs to be **seen through**.

The Nature of Devotion

In this chapter, Krishna also speaks of four kinds of devotees—those who seek help in distress, those who seek wealth, the inquisitive, and the wise.

Shankara sees these as **stages of evolution**. Each expresses devotion, but only the wise (*Jñānī Bhakta*) truly knows the Divine as the Self.

For Shankara, **Bhakti and Jñāna are not separate paths**. Bhakti is steadfast contemplation of one's own Self as Brahman; it matures into non-dual realization.

"The devotee who sees no distinction between himself and Brahman
loves truly, for love then is oneness."
— *Shankara, Gita Bhāṣya 7.17*

The Rare Jewel of Wisdom

Krishna proclaims:

"Among thousands of men, one may strive for perfection; among the perfected, perhaps one truly knows Me."
— *Bhagavad Gita 7.3*

Shankara comments that true realization is rare not because it is distant, but because few persevere to dissolve the ego completely. Most stop at intellectual understanding; few surrender the knower itself.

The *Jñānī*—the knower of truth—is compared to a flame that no wind can disturb. He does not merely know that Brahman exists; he **lives as Brahman itself**.

Philosophical Summary: Jñāna Vijñāna Yoga

According to Shankara's Advaitic interpretation:

- **Jñāna** is discriminative knowledge—the understanding that Brahman alone is real.
- **Vijñāna** is the direct, continuous experience of that truth in all situations.
- **Apara Prakṛti** (lower nature) is the field of appearances;
  Para Prakṛti (higher nature) is consciousness itself.
- **Māyā** veils unity and projects diversity.
- **Bhakti** is the love that arises when all separation dissolves.

In this way, knowledge becomes devotion, and devotion becomes knowledge—two sides of the same awakening.

Reflections for the Seeker

1. **Move from Information to Illumination**
   Let study become introspection, and introspection become vision. True knowing transforms the knower.

2. **See the Divine in All Forms**
   Whether in beauty or hardship, recognize the same consciousness shining through every experience.
3. **Understand and Transcend Māyā**
   Don't battle illusion—see it for what it is, a play of perception upon the changeless Self.
4. **Let Love Mature into Knowledge**
   Devotion that begins with longing must end in identity: "I am That."

Conclusion: Knowledge Blossoming as Wisdom

Through Shankara's eyes, *Jñāna Vijñāna Yoga* is the moment when understanding becomes illumination.

The seeker no longer reaches toward the Divine but awakens as the Divine.

The study of Brahman concludes in silence—where words cease, and being alone speaks.

"When knowledge ripens into direct realization,
the knower, knowledge, and known are one—
the eternal Self, shining without a second."
— *Adi Shankaracharya*

The Imperishable Absolute

That which the knowers of the Vedas call the Imperishable,
which the ascetics enter, desiring freedom—
that state I shall declare unto you.
— *Bhagavad Gita 8.11*

The Mystery of the Eternal

This chapter opens with Arjuna's inquiry into the ultimate truth:

"What is Brahman? What is the Self? What is Karma? What is the field of sacrifice?"

Here, Krishna leads the seeker into one of the most profound contemplations of the *Gita*—the realization of **Akṣara Brahman**, the Imperishable Reality that transcends birth and death.

For **Ādi Shankaracharya**, this chapter illuminates the **timeless dimension of knowledge**—that which is beyond cause, beyond decay, beyond duality.

While previous teachings prepared the mind through knowledge, devotion, and meditation, this chapter unveils the *goal itself*: the Eternal that neither arises nor ceases.

Shankara's Interpretation: Brahman Beyond Time

In his *Bhāṣya*, Shankara defines *Akṣara Brahman* as the **absolute, unchanging consciousness**—the substratum of all existence.

It is *imperishable* because it is not produced, does not transform, and cannot perish.

"Brahman is that which remains ever the same—
the witness of all changes, untouched by the seen or the seer."
— *Shankara, Gita Bhāṣya 8.3*

This imperishable Self, he says, is not separate from the individual Self (*Ātman*). The difference arises only from ignorance. Once that veil falls away, one realizes that the finite self has never been apart from the infinite.

Thus, the chapter is not about reaching some distant realm after death, but about recognizing **deathlessness here and now**.

The Knowledge of the Unborn

Krishna describes Brahman as the **eternal ground of all beings**—that into which the universe dissolves and from which it arises again.

"At the coming of day, all beings manifest;
at the coming of night, they dissolve into the unmanifest."
— *Bhagavad Gita 8.18*

Shankara interprets this cyclical vision cosmologically and spiritually.

Cosmologically, it refers to the creation and dissolution of worlds; spiritually, it mirrors the awakening and sleep of consciousness in the individual.

Just as sleep conceals but does not destroy the waking mind, so the dissolution of the universe conceals but does not destroy Brahman. The imperishable remains ever untouched—*the witnessing awareness through all beginnings and endings.*

The Moment of Death and the Power of Remembrance

One of the most moving portions of this chapter concerns the **final remembrance** at the time of death.

"At the time of death, he who remembers Me alone, leaving the body,
goes forth to My being; there is no doubt of this."
— *Bhagavad Gita 8.5*

Shankara clarifies that remembrance (*Smaraṇa*) here does not mean mechanical repetition but **steady awareness of identity with the Self**.
If a lifetime has been spent in meditation and self-knowledge, the final moment simply continues that awareness without break.

Thus, liberation is not a posthumous event; it is the **culmination of conscious living**. Death merely reveals what has already been realized.

For Shankara, the last thought determines the next birth only for those still ignorant of their true nature. For the wise, there is no "next"—only timeless being.

The Two Paths: Light and Darkness

Krishna describes two cosmic paths—the *bright path* leading to liberation and the *dark path* leading to return.

"Fire, light, daytime, the bright fortnight, the six months of the sun's northern course—
those who know Brahman, departing then, go to the Supreme."
— *Bhagavad Gita 8.24*

Shankara interprets these not as literal astronomical events but as **symbols of inner states**.
The "bright path" represents clarity, knowledge, and upward movement of consciousness.
The "dark path" represents ignorance and attachment, binding the soul to rebirth.

The enlightened one transcends both. For him, the very distinction of path dissolves, for **Brahman is beyond direction, space, and time.**

The Eternal Witness

Shankara repeatedly emphasizes that the *Akṣara Brahman* is **not reached**—it is ever-present.

All paths, practices, and meditations culminate in this recognition: the witness of all experience is itself the goal.

The imperishable is not somewhere else, nor in the future.

It is **that which is aware even of the thought of time**.

"That which illumines waking, dream, and deep sleep,
yet is not limited by any of them—
that is Brahman, the imperishable."
— *Shankara, Vivekachudamani*

The Nature of True Immortality

For Shankara, immortality does not mean endless continuity of existence as an individual; rather, it means freedom from the illusion of individuality.

Death is only the dissolution of the body and mind, not of consciousness.

The one who knows this **sees death as a shadow**, not an end.

To such a sage, every moment is eternity, for he dwells in that which neither comes nor goes.

This is the true *Amṛtatva*—immortality not of time, but of timeless awareness.

Philosophical Summary: Akṣara Brahma Yoga

Shankara's Advaitic synthesis of this chapter may be distilled as follows:

- **Akṣara Brahman** is the imperishable consciousness, the Self of all.

- **Death** pertains only to body and mind; the Self is unborn and undecaying.
- **Remembrance of Brahman** at death reflects lifelong realization.
- **The bright and dark paths** symbolize knowledge and ignorance.
- **Immortality** is not continuation but transcendence of individuality.

When ignorance ends, the knower merges in Brahman—not by movement, but by recognition of unity.

Reflections for the Seeker

1. **Contemplate the Imperishable**
   Amid all changes, return again and again to the awareness that watches them. That awareness never changes.
2. **Practice Constant Remembrance**
   Let every breath become remembrance of the Self—not as a concept, but as direct presence.
3. **Transcend the Fear of Death**
   Death touches only what is born. The witnessing consciousness was never born; it cannot die.
4. **Dwell in the Eternal Now**
   The Akṣara is not found after death but in the timeless stillness of the present.

Conclusion: The Deathless Light

For **Ādi Shankaracharya**, *Akṣara Brahma Yoga* is not a doctrine of the afterlife but a revelation of the ever-present. The seeker who knows the Self as Akṣara no longer lives *in* time—he lives *as* eternity itself.

This is the knowledge that frees not tomorrow, but now; not in heaven, but here.

"The imperishable is not attained by going anywhere,
but by ceasing to go.
It is known when the knower rests in the knowing itself."
— *Adi Shankaracharya*

The Royal Knowledge and the Royal Secret

This is the royal knowledge, the royal secret, the supreme purifier, easily practicable, imperishable, and sweet in its result.
— *Bhagavad Gita 9.2*

The Inner Revelation

Having illumined the imperishable nature of Brahman in the previous chapter, Krishna now discloses the **crown of all wisdom** — the *Rāja Vidyā*, the king of knowledge, and *Rāja Guhya*, the king of secrets.

For **Ādi Shankaracharya**, this chapter represents **the heart of the Gita's Advaitic revelation**: the direct realization that Brahman is both the immanent essence within the universe and the transcendent reality beyond it. Knowledge becomes royal because it reveals the **sovereignty of the Self**, and secret because it can only be grasped through inner purity, not through intellect alone.

Shankara's Interpretation: The Secret of Non-Dual Devotion

In his *Bhāṣya*, Shankara explains that the "royal secret" lies in recognizing that **devotion (*Bhakti*) and knowledge (*Jñāna*) are one**. The supreme devotion Krishna describes here is not emotional worship but **constant contemplation of one's identity with the Divine**.

"He who sees no difference between himself and the Lord, and loves thus — his devotion is knowledge itself."
— *Shankara, Gita Bhāṣya 9.22*

In the earlier chapters, knowledge led to detachment; here, knowledge blossoms into love. The realization "I am Brahman" matures into the silent reverence that sees Brahman in all.

The Divine Immanence

Krishna declares:

"All this world is pervaded by Me in My unmanifest form; all beings dwell in Me, yet I do not dwell in them."
— *Bhagavad Gita 9.4*

This paradox finds its solution in Shankara's commentary: Brahman is the **substratum of all phenomena**, yet remains unaffected by them — like space, within which all forms arise and dissolve without altering the space itself.

To the ignorant, the Divine appears hidden; to the wise, **the Divine is all there is**. This is the royal vision: not worshipping God as separate, but recognizing **the Self as the only reality** appearing as the cosmos.

The Play of Māyā

"The foolish disregard Me when I appear in human form; not knowing My higher being, supreme and imperishable."
— *Bhagavad Gita 9.11*

Shankara explains that those bound by *Māyā* perceive only the limited form of the Divine — the historical Krishna, the finite teacher. The wise perceive through the form the formless essence, as one sees the ocean in every wave.

Māyā veils, but does not confine. Once the veil of duality thins, the seeker perceives the eternal Brahman shining through every appearance.

The Law of Faith

Krishna speaks of those who worship various deities, explaining that faith itself has power, but its fruit remains limited to the realm of becoming.

Shankara clarifies that all worship ultimately reaches Brahman, for **Brahman alone receives every offering**, though the ignorant do not perceive it. When devotion is directed to any form, it is Brahman who accepts it — the forms are but channels.

However, **the fruit corresponds to the understanding**: those who see separation reap finite results; those who see unity reap liberation.

The Universal Embrace

One of the most compassionate proclamations of the Gita appears here:

"Even if the most sinful worships Me with undivided devotion,
he must be regarded as righteous, for he has rightly resolved."
— *Bhagavad Gita 9.30*

Shankara's insight is deeply psychological. The transformative power of single-pointed devotion (*Ananya Bhakti*) purifies instantly, because it uproots the ego — the source of all sin. When the ego dissolves, what remains is purity itself.

Thus, the Lord excludes none. Even one fallen in conduct but sincere in heart attains peace through steadfast remembrance of the Self.

The Synthesis of Knowledge and Love

Shankara's Advaita never separates head from heart. Here, he declares that the culmination of knowledge is **love without**

ove that arises when the lover, beloved, and love nized as one.

nowledge is therefore not academic or ritualistic, **tial**. It transforms life into worship, perception on, and every act into offering.

l beings in Me and Myself in all beings—
knowledge, for in that vision all division ends."
a, Gita Bhāṣya 9.29

sophical Summary: Rāja Vidyā Rāja Guhya

ara's Advaitic summary of this chapter:

- **Rāja Vidyā** is knowledge of the non-dual Self, sovereign over all sciences.
- **Rāja Guhya** is its secret nature—realized only through purity and devotion.
- **Brahman** pervades all beings yet remains untouched.
- **Māyā** makes the infinite appear finite, the one appear as many.
- **Bhakti (Jñāna-Bhakti)** is unwavering contemplation of one's identity with Brahman.
- **Grace** is the natural flow of realization, not a favor bestowed.

Thus, the chapter synthesizes **knowledge, devotion, and grace** into a single current flowing toward the ocean of unity.

Reflections for the Seeker

1. **Let Knowledge Become Reverence**
   When understanding deepens into wonder, wisdom becomes sacred.

2. **See God in All**
   The Divine hides in plain sight—as lig
   thought, and breath.
3. **Transcend Judgment**
   The purest devotion may arise from the hu
   heart; seek sincerity, not perfection.
4. **Live as Offering**
   When every action is consecrated to the Whole,
   itself becomes worship.

Conclusion: The Heart of Non-Dual Love

For **Ādi Shankaracharya**, *Rāja Vidyā Rāja Guhya Yoga* reveals the **final intimacy between the human and the divine**. The seeker discovers that the secret long hidden was never distant—it was the Self, silently watching through all experiences.

Here, love and wisdom fuse; devotion becomes realization; the worshipper and the worshipped vanish into oneness.

"He who knows this secret need not seek the Divine elsewhere;
for the seeker, the seeking, and the sought are one—
the royal knowledge, the royal secret."
— *Adi Shankaracharya*

The Yoga of Divine Glories

I am the Self, O Gudākesha, seated in the hearts of all beings;
I am the beginning, the middle, and also the end of all.
— *Bhagavad Gita 10.20*

The Universe as Revelation

Having unveiled the royal knowledge of oneness, Krishna now unfolds the **cosmic panorama** of that oneness in manifestation.

The tenth chapter is a hymn of wonder — a vision of the Divine shining through every aspect of existence.

For **Ādi Shankaracharya**, *Vibhūti Yoga* is not a catalogue of supernatural powers or mythic spectacles, but a **meditation on the omnipresence of Brahman**. Each glory Krishna names — whether a mountain, river, sage, or virtue — is a symbol pointing to the truth that **there is no place where the Infinite is not**.

Shankara's Interpretation: Seeing the One in the Many

In his *Bhāṣya*, Shankara clarifies that Krishna enumerates His manifestations to **turn the seeker's attention outward only to lead it inward**.

By recognizing the Divine in the most exalted expressions of the world — strength in the strong, wisdom in the wise, light in the luminous — the seeker begins to perceive the single consciousness underlying diversity.

"Wherever there is excellence, power, or glory,
know it to spring from a fraction of My splendor."
— *Bhagavad Gita 10.41*

Thus, *Vibhūti Yoga* becomes **a contemplative exercise in universal recognition**: the mind that once divided life into sacred and profane learns to see all as sacred.

The Nature of the Manifested Divine

Krishna declares Himself as:

- Vishnu among the Ādityas,
- the radiant Sun among lights,
- the Mind among the senses,
- the Himalayas among immovable things,
- the syllable *Om* among words,
- and Consciousness among beings.

Shankara explains that these examples represent **the most expressive points of perception**, through which the Infinite hints its presence. The mountain reveals steadfastness, the river reveals flow, *Om* reveals vibration — all are metaphors for the **same silent awareness** that pervades everything.

These glories are not separate from the Absolute; they are its **play (*Līlā*)** — the Infinite reflecting itself in the finite.

From Admiration to Absorption

Arjuna listens, overwhelmed by this vastness, his heart filled with devotion. Krishna's intention, Shankara remarks, is to **transform admiration into meditation**.

When the mind contemplates the Divine not as distant but as the very essence of all experience, it becomes serene and expansive.

This is the practical power of *Vibhūti Yoga*: every perception becomes a doorway to the Eternal. Seeing beauty, strength, intelligence, or virtue anywhere becomes a moment of worship.

"When the intellect is purified by perceiving the Divine in all things,
it naturally turns inward to the source of all splendor."
— *Shankara, Gita Bhāṣya 10.42*

The Infinite in a Single Spark

Krishna concludes:

"With a single portion of Myself, I sustain this entire universe."
— *Bhagavad Gita 10.42*

Shankara expounds: this verse reveals the **measureless nature of Brahman**.
All worlds, gods, and beings arise from a mere reflection of the Infinite — just as the sun's image dances in countless waters without dividing the sun itself.

The purpose of this teaching is not to expand theology but to **contract the ego**.
When one realizes that every form is a spark of the same flame, pride dissolves, and only reverence remains.

The Spiritual Psychology of Wonder

Shankara beautifully notes that **awe is the threshold of realization**.
Wonder purifies intellect because it silences thought.
To stand amazed before existence — seeing the play of the One in all — is to stand at the door of enlightenment.

When perception becomes wonder, and wonder becomes silence, the seeker awakens to the **Vibhūti within** — the limitless consciousness that gives meaning to all manifestations.

Philosophical Summary: Vibhūti Yoga

According to Shankara's Advaitic interpretation:

- **Vibhūtis** are manifestations of Brahman's glory in the field of illusion.
- The purpose of enumerating them is **meditative recognition**, not worship of multiplicity.
- **The One becomes many** through *Māyā*, yet remains untouched.
- True devotion is **seeing the Divine in all excellence** and returning inward to the unmanifest source.
- Every quality, power, or beauty is a **pointer to the Self**, not apart from it.

Thus, the external splendor is an invitation to discover the **inner brilliance**.

Reflections for the Seeker

1. **Turn Admiration into Meditation**
   Whenever something inspires you, trace that feeling back to the silent witness within — the same presence shining through the object of wonder.
2. **See Divinity in Diversity**
   The countless forms of life are not distractions from the truth; they are expressions of it.
3. **Let Humility Arise from Grandeur**
   Recognize the infinite operating through every power — in that recognition, ego melts.
4. **Live in Continuous Reverence**
   Make every encounter, sound, and sight a reminder of the Divine that pervades all.

Conclusion: The Light Behind All Lights

For **Ādi Shankaracharya**, *Vibhūti Yoga* is the art of perceiving **Brahman in manifestation**.

When the mind ceases to divide the world into sacred and ordinary, it begins to perceive divinity everywhere — in the rising sun, in the silence between thoughts, in the very breath of awareness.

The royal secret of the previous chapter becomes here the **royal vision**: to know that every splendor is His and that the Self of all beings is the same Self.

"When all forms are known as His forms,
and all powers as His powers,
the seer rests in the powerless, formless One —
the glory beyond all glories."
— *Adi Shankaracharya*

The Vision of the Cosmic Form

Behold, O Arjuna, My forms manifold, divine, of various colors and shapes;
behold the entire universe, moving and unmoving, concentrated here in My body.
— *Bhagavad Gita 11.5–7*

The Moment of Revelation

The *Vibhūti Yoga* opened Arjuna's heart to perceive divinity within the manifold of creation. Now, in the **Viśvarūpa Darśana Yoga**, Krishna removes the final veil, granting Arjuna the direct **vision of the entire cosmos as one boundless, living form**.

For **Ādi Shankaracharya**, this vision does not reveal something *new*; rather, it **unveils the already-present truth** that all multiplicity is contained within the One Consciousness. The cosmic form is the grand metaphor of **non-dual realization** — the understanding that there is nothing outside the Divine.

Shankara's Interpretation: The Vision of Oneness

In his *Bhāṣya*, Shankara explains that the **Viśvarūpa (Universal Form)** is a divinely granted perception (*Yoga-aiśvarya*), made possible through Krishna's grace. It represents the **total manifestation of Brahman through Māyā** — the Infinite appearing as the totality of names and forms.

"The Lord's cosmic form is not apart from Brahman,
yet it belongs to the realm of the empirical —
the vision is within the world of appearance,
but the Truth it reveals is beyond appearance."
— *Shankara, Gita Bhāṣya 11.8*

Shankara clarifies that this vision is not necessary for enlightenment; it is **a symbolic initiation into Advaitic awareness**. Arjuna's eyes are divinely empowered so he may perceive the Absolute manifest as the relative.

The Divine Eye

Krishna says:

"You cannot see Me with your physical eyes;
I grant you divine vision — behold My majestic yoga!"
— *Bhagavad Gita 11.8*

Shankara interprets this "divine vision" (*Divya Chakṣu*) as **the eye of knowledge**, purified by grace and prepared by meditation. It is not a physical transformation but a **shift of consciousness** — from perceiving parts to perceiving the Whole.

In this vision, all distinctions of form, time, and space collapse into a single pulsating presence — infinite, terrible, and beautiful.

The Awe of the Infinite

Arjuna beholds the unimaginable: countless faces, eyes, and mouths; beings entering and emerging; universes blazing and dissolving in the fire of Krishna's glory.

Shankara remarks that this vision is meant to **shatter the ego's illusion of control**. Arjuna, who hesitated to fight his kin, now sees that all beings are already instruments in the cosmic order — that life and death, creation and destruction, are movements of the same Reality.

"I am Time, the mighty destroyer, come to consume the worlds."
— *Bhagavad Gita 11.32*

For Shankara, *Kāla* (Time) here represents **the dynamic aspect of Brahman**, through which all events unfold. The finite trembles before this vision because it reveals the truth that nothing stands apart from the eternal process.

The Collapse of Duality

Overwhelmed, Arjuna bows in reverence, trembling with awe. He sees both the terrible and the tender within the same form — the destroyer and the sustainer, the terrifying and the compassionate.

Shankara teaches that this experience mirrors the **seeker's confrontation with the Absolute**: when the ego dissolves, the dualities of good and evil, beauty and horror, life and death merge into a single reality.

The mind, accustomed to opposites, collapses in silence. Only the witness remains.

This is not the end of knowledge but the beginning of **wisdom through surrender**.

From Vision to Devotion

Arjuna, unable to bear the immensity of the universal form, begs Krishna to return to His gentle, human aspect. Krishna complies, revealing again the **twofold nature of the Divine**: the unmanifest Absolute and its merciful manifestation as the personal Lord.

Shankara notes that this transformation symbolizes the **return from the transcendental to the immanent**, from the cosmic to the intimate. The seeker who has glimpsed unity learns to reengage with the world, seeing the Divine in all beings, not apart from them.

"He who sees Me everywhere, and everything in Me, never loses sight of Me, nor do I of him."
— *Bhagavad Gita 6.30*

The *Viśvarūpa* vision, therefore, concludes not in fear but in **love** — a devotion born of understanding, where the universe is no longer an obstacle but a revelation.

Philosophical Summary: Viśvarūpa Darśana Yoga

According to Shankara's Advaitic interpretation:

- **The Cosmic Vision** is a symbolic revelation of the unity of all existence within Brahman.
- **Divine Vision** (*Divya Chakṣu*) represents purified perception — seeing through Māyā.
- **The Terrible Aspect** of the Divine reveals the illusory nature of individual control.
- **The Gentle Aspect** restores relational love once knowledge of unity is established.
- **The Vision** itself belongs to the realm of empirical perception (*Vyavahāra*), while the truth it points to is absolute (*Pāramārthika*).

The *Viśvarūpa* thus serves as the bridge between perception and realization — between the world of appearance and the Self that transcends it.

Reflections for the Seeker

1. **Open the Inner Eye**
   The divine eye is awareness itself — the ability to see unity amidst diversity. Cultivate it through meditation and discernment.

2. **Surrender to the Vastness**
   Let awe dissolve arrogance. The infinite is not against you; it is you, without boundary.
3. **Recognize Time as the Divine**
   Do not fear change — it is Brahman moving through forms. The eternal wears the face of impermanence.
4. **Return to Compassion**
   After glimpsing oneness, serve all beings as embodiments of the same Self. Vision matures into love.

Conclusion: The Universe as the Self

For **Ādi Shankaracharya**, *Viśvarūpa Darśana Yoga* is the *drama of awakening*. The seeker sees the Absolute as the universe, then as the Self within.

What begins as spectacle ends as silence; what begins as multitude ends as One.

The cosmic vision is not meant to astonish but to liberate — to awaken the realization that **the same consciousness that beholds the universe is the universe itself**.

"When the seer and the seen are known to be one,
all fear ends, all searching ceases —
only the Self remains, boundless and bright."
— *Adi Shankaracharya*

The Yoga of Devotion

Those who, ever steadfast, worship Me with single-minded devotion,
I lift them up from the ocean of mortality.
— *Bhagavad Gita 12.6–7*

The Heart of Realization

After the overwhelming vision of the *Viśvarūpa*, Arjuna turns inward and asks a question that lives at the heart of spiritual inquiry:

"Who are better — those who worship You in form, or those who meditate upon the formless, imperishable Brahman?"
— *Bhagavad Gita 12.1*

In his commentary, **Ādi Shankaracharya** interprets this as the natural progression from **vision to understanding** — from the cosmic to the personal, from awe to intimacy.

For Shankara, *Bhakti Yoga* is not a new path apart from knowledge, but **the flowering of knowledge into love**. When the intellect has realized unity, the heart overflows in devotion.

Shankara's Interpretation: Bhakti as Steady Knowledge

Shankara defines *Bhakti* as **constant contemplation on one's own true nature as Brahman**, not emotional worship or ritual adoration.

"Bhakti is unwavering meditation upon the Self as the Supreme Reality —
the love born of knowledge that nothing else exists."
— *Shankara, Gita Bhāṣya 12.2*

Those who worship the formless Brahman, he explains, tread a steep and subtle path requiring immense discipline and dispassion. Those who love the Divine through form begin with duality, but their love matures into non-dual awareness when they see **the same Lord in all beings**.

Thus, devotion and knowledge converge like two rivers flowing into the ocean of realization.

The Path of the Devotee

Krishna describes the qualities of the true devotee:

- Free from hatred toward any being,
- Friendly and compassionate,
- Without ego,
- Content and forgiving,
- Ever self-controlled,
- Steadfast in faith.

Shankara notes that these are not external disciplines but **natural expressions of realized understanding**. The devotee's compassion arises because he no longer perceives "others." His humility comes from seeing the same Self shining in all.

"The highest devotion is not a relationship with God,
but identity with the Self of all beings."
— *Shankara, Gita Bhāṣya 12.13–14*

The Nature of Divine Love

In *Bhakti Yoga*, Krishna introduces the concept of **Ananya Bhakti** — exclusive devotion.

This is not narrowness of faith, but **freedom from duality**. The devotee clings to nothing outside the Divine because he has recognized that nothing is outside the Divine.

Shankara emphasizes that this devotion is not sentiment but **stability of awareness**. The mind, freed from distraction, rests in its own source — in the Self.

Love here is not desire for union; it is **recognition that there was never separation**.

The Formless and the Form

Krishna explains that worship of the formless Brahman is difficult for those identified with body and senses. Shankara agrees, explaining that the mind, being attached to form, struggles to conceive the unmanifest.

Therefore, worship through form — through the personal God (*Īśvara*) — serves as a compassionate bridge. The form becomes a **mirror** reflecting the formless. When the reflection is understood as light itself, form dissolves naturally into essence.

In this way, personal devotion (*Saguna Bhakti*) ripens into knowledge of the Impersonal (*Nirguna Jñāna*).

Surrender as Wisdom

"Fix your mind on Me alone, let your intellect dwell in Me; thereafter you shall live in Me, no doubt remains."

— *Bhagavad Gita 12.8*

Shankara explains this as the final synthesis of the *Gita*:

To fix the mind on the Lord means to **rest awareness in the Self**, the eternal witness of all thoughts.

To surrender the intellect means to let go of identification with doership.

Thus, *Śaraṇāgati* (surrender) is not submission to an external deity but the **dissolution of ego in knowledge** — a letting-go into the truth that "I am That."

"Surrender and knowledge are not two;
when the ego ends, surrender and wisdom are one act."
— *Shankara*

The Devotee Beyond Comparison

Krishna concludes this chapter by describing the devotee who is "dear to Him."

He is fearless, pure, silent, and detached from outcomes. He is content with whatever comes, unmoved by joy or sorrow, gain or loss.

Shankara observes that such equanimity is the **fragrance of realization**.

Devotion here does not depend on emotion or ritual — it is the spontaneous stillness of a liberated mind.

The true devotee loves not *for* something, but *as* love itself — limitless, formless, and self-luminous.

Philosophical Summary: Bhakti Yoga

In Shankara's Advaitic exposition:

- **Bhakti** is steadfast contemplation of one's identity with Brahman.
- **Devotion through form** matures into realization of the formless.
- **Surrender** is the relinquishment of ego, not of understanding.
- **The qualities of the devotee** arise naturally from self-knowledge.
- **Love and knowledge** are not two paths but two aspects of one truth.

Thus, *Bhakti Yoga* is **Jñāna made fragrant by love** — the serenity of understanding expressed as compassion for all beings.

Reflections for the Seeker

1. **Let Knowledge Soften into Love**
   Understanding without tenderness is incomplete. Let realization flow into the heart.
2. **See God in Everyone**
   Every being is a doorway to the Divine. Treat all as sacred mirrors of your own Self.
3. **Practice Inner Surrender**
   Offer the sense of "I" into awareness. Let action happen without ownership.
4. **Be Silent in Love**
   When devotion matures, words become unnecessary; being itself becomes prayer.

Conclusion: Love as the Face of Wisdom

For **Ādi Shankaracharya**, *Bhakti Yoga* is not apart from the path of knowledge — it is its fulfillment.
After knowing that all is Brahman, the heart naturally bows in reverence to all.

This is **the highest devotion**: the serene love that arises when there is no "other" left to love.

"When the lover, the loved, and love itself dissolve into the Self,
that is Bhakti — the peace of non-duality."
— *Adi Shankaracharya*

Distinction Between Field and Knower of Field

This body, O Kaunteya, is called the field;
he who knows it is called the knower of the field.
Know Me also as the knower in all fields.
— *Bhagavad Gita 13.1–2*

The Science of Self-Awareness

With this chapter, the *Gita* enters its **metaphysical summit**.

Here, Krishna introduces the timeless distinction between the **Field (*Kṣetra*)**, which is everything that can be known, and the **Knower of the Field (*Kṣetrajña*)**, pure consciousness itself.

For **Ādi Shankaracharya**, this teaching is the *pivot* of Advaita Vedānta.

It draws the clear line between **the transient and the eternal**, between **the object of knowledge and the subject that never changes**.

All previous yogas—of action, devotion, and meditation—prepare the seeker for this discriminative insight (*Viveka*).

Shankara's Interpretation: The Field Is Not the Self

In his *Bhāṣya*, Shankara explains:

- The *Kṣetra* (field) comprises the **body, mind, senses, and all phenomena**—everything subject to change, decay, and perception.
- The *Kṣetrajña* (knower of the field) is **consciousness itself**—the witness of all experience, unchanging and eternal.

"The field is that which is known; the knower is the light of awareness.
To mistake the field for the knower is the bondage of ignorance."
— *Shankara, Gita Bhāṣya 13.2*

Thus, liberation is the recognition that *I am not the field*—not body, mind, or thought—but **the pure knower of them all**.

The Field (Kṣetra): The Domain of Change

Krishna enumerates the components of the field: the five elements, the ego, intellect, mind, the senses, desire, aversion, pleasure, pain, the body, and life force.

Shankara calls this the **apparatus of experience**—a composite of matter and mind animated by consciousness.
He compares it to a city governed by a silent witness; the field performs countless activities, but the knower remains untouched.

The *Kṣetra* is not evil; it is **the play of Māyā**, the canvas upon which the drama of life unfolds. Yet mistaking this field for the Self is the root of suffering.

The Knower (Kṣetrajña): The Witness Beyond Change

"Know that I am the knower in all fields."
— *Bhagavad Gita 13.3*

This statement, Shankara declares, is the essence of non-dualism.
There are not many knowers—there is **one consciousness** reflected in countless minds, like the sun mirrored in many pools.

When one mind realizes its true nature, it recognizes that the light within is the same light everywhere.

Thus, the individual self (*Jīva*) and the cosmic self (*Īśvara*) are not two; they are one reality, viewed through the lenses of ignorance and knowledge respectively.

The Union of Knowledge and Experience

Krishna next describes the qualities that prepare the seeker for realization:
humility, non-violence, patience, sincerity, detachment from sense pleasures, steadiness, and love of solitude.

Shankara notes that these virtues (*Jñāna-sādhanāni*) are not moral prescriptions but **inner disciplines** that make the mind transparent.
Only a tranquil mind can reflect truth clearly.
When agitation ceases, knowledge dawns effortlessly—like the moon reflected on still water.

Knowing the Known and the Knower

"That which is to be known I shall declare—
by knowing which one attains immortality.
It is beginningless, supreme Brahman,
said to be neither being nor non-being."
— *Bhagavad Gita 13.12–13*

Shankara explains that Brahman, the ultimate reality, transcends both existence and non-existence as we conceive them. It is not an object among objects, but the **illumining principle** that makes all knowing possible.

To "know" Brahman, therefore, is to **abide as awareness itself**, free from identification with the field.

The All-Pervading Light

Krishna describes Brahman as:

"hands and feet everywhere, eyes, heads, mouths, and ears everywhere;
pervading all things, He stands embracing all."

Shankara interprets this poetically: the Lord has hands wherever there is action, eyes wherever there is sight, intelligence wherever there is thought.
Brahman is **immanent in every faculty**, yet transcendent as the witness of all faculties.

"He shines by Himself, and through His light all things shine."
— *Shankara, Gita Bhāṣya 13.17*

This verse captures the Advaitic revelation: consciousness is not *in* the world—the world appears *in* consciousness.

The Meeting of Purusha and Prakṛti

Krishna teaches that *Prakṛti* (Nature) and *Puruṣa* (Spirit) are without beginning.
From their union arise all beings and experiences.

Shankara distinguishes:

- *Prakṛti* is the **power of manifestation**, the principle of change;
- *Puruṣa* is **unchanging consciousness**, the silent witness.

Ignorance causes identification with *Prakṛti* ("I act, I enjoy, I suffer").
Knowledge reveals that the Self is not the doer but the observer—*the screen, not the movie.*

When this understanding becomes direct and constant, bondage ends.

The Vision of the Wise

"He who sees the Supreme Lord dwelling equally in all beings,
the imperishable amid the perishing, truly sees."
— *Bhagavad Gita 13.27*

Shankara comments that this is **the culmination of Advaita**.
Seeing equality everywhere means recognizing that consciousness—the knower—is one and the same in all beings.
Individual distinctions are but modifications of the field; the knower remains untouched, unbroken, unbounded.

This is the state of liberation (*Jīvanmukti*)—living free while still embodied.

Philosophical Summary: Kṣetra Kṣetrajña Vibhāga Yoga

Shankara's non-dual synthesis of this chapter:

- **Kṣetra** is the body-mind complex and all objects of experience.
- **Kṣetrajña** is pure consciousness, the eternal witness.
- **Ignorance** binds consciousness to the field through identification.
- **Knowledge** reveals that consciousness alone is real; the field is appearance.
- **Liberation** is abidance in the knower, not destruction of the field.

Thus, wisdom is not withdrawal from life but seeing life as a play upon the screen of awareness.

Reflections for the Seeker

1. **Discern the Seer from the Seen**
   Pause often and notice: "This thought, this feeling, this body—I am aware of them. Therefore, I am not them."
2. **Recognize One Consciousness in All**
   Every being you meet looks through the same window of awareness. See yourself in all eyes.
3. **Let Stillness Be Your Practice**
   When the mind grows quiet, the field fades, and the knower shines self-evident.
4. **Live in the World, Unentangled**
   Act through the field, but rest as the witness. Engagement without attachment is freedom.

Conclusion: The Light That Knows Itself

For **Ādi Shankaracharya**, *Kṣetra Kṣetrajña Vibhāga Yoga* is the **essence of Advaita Vedānta** distilled into the dialogue of teacher and disciple.

Here, the *Gita* ceases to be a philosophy of doing and becomes a revelation of being.

When the field is known as appearance and the knower as pure reality, the seeker awakens to the truth:

the observer of all is the only existence there is.

"He who knows the difference between the field and the knower

sees not two but the one Self—

the witness of all fields, untouched, eternal."

— *Adi Shankaracharya*

The Division of the Three Guṇas

Knowledge, action, and the doer are declared by the sages to be of three kinds,
according to the distinction of the guṇas born of Nature.
— *Bhagavad Gita 14.5*

The Thread of Nature

After explaining the field and its knower, Krishna now unfolds the *texture* of the field itself — the three *guṇas*, or fundamental strands of *Prakṛti* (Nature): **Sattva** (illumination), **Rajas** (activity), and **Tamas** (inertia).

For **Ādi Shankaracharya**, this teaching reveals **the subtle mechanism of bondage**.
The *guṇas* are not moral categories but **energetic tendencies** through which the unchanging consciousness experiences the ever-changing world.
They weave together body, mind, and cosmos — binding the eternal witness to the play of becoming.

Shankara's View: Guṇas as the Fabric of Māyā

In his *Bhāṣya*, Shankara explains that the *guṇas* belong wholly to *Prakṛti*, never to the *Ātman*.
They are the **threads of illusion** that spin the web of individuality.

"The guṇas revolve within the guṇas;
the wise know this and remain unattached."
— *Shankara, Gita Bhāṣya 14.19*

To understand them is to see how Nature functions independently of the Self.

Just as clouds move through the sky without touching it, so thoughts, desires, and moods — products of the *guṇas* — arise and subside without altering awareness.

Sattva — The Guṇa of Illumination

Sattva is purity, harmony, and light.

It binds through **attachment to happiness and knowledge**.

Even though refined, it is still bondage, because identification with joy or virtue sustains subtle ego.

Shankara likens Sattva to a golden chain — more pleasant than Rajas or Tamas, yet still a chain.

Its function is to **prepare the mind for liberation** by clarifying perception and lessening restlessness.

Rajas — The Guṇa of Activity

Rajas arises from desire. It impels movement, effort, and ambition, binding through **attachment to action and its fruits**.

The rajasic mind is ever-outward-turned, seeking fulfillment in achievement and recognition.

Shankara warns that Rajas perpetuates the illusion of doership — the sense of "I act."

Until this identification dissolves, the Self remains veiled.

Tamas — The Guṇa of Inertia

Tamas, born of ignorance, obscures awareness through sloth, confusion, and delusion.

It binds by **neglect, indifference, and sleep** — both literal and spiritual.

Yet Shankara notes that even Tamas serves a function: it provides rest after the exhaustion of Rajas and prepares the mind to return toward Sattva.

Thus, the *guṇas* interact ceaselessly, balancing one another in Nature's eternal rhythm.

The Play of the Guṇas

Krishna explains that all beings are governed by the interplay of these three forces.

Sattva brings clarity; Rajas, agitation; Tamas, dullness.

Shankara comments that **the Self is never touched by any of them**.

When the seeker perceives that the *guṇas* act within the *guṇas* alone — that is, when activity is seen as belonging to Nature, not to the Self — the knots of karma loosen, and the witness stands free.

"He who knows 'the guṇas alone act'
and remains unmoved, he verily knows."
— *Shankara, Gita Bhāṣya 14.23*

Transcending the Three

Arjuna asks how one rises beyond the *guṇas*.

Krishna replies:

"He who is alike in honor and dishonor,
the same in friend and foe,
who renounces all undertakings—
he has transcended the guṇas."
— *Bhagavad Gita 14.25*

Shankara explains that transcendence does not destroy the *guṇas*; it destroys **identification with them**.

The liberated one does not seek to control Nature but **ceases to mistake himself for Nature**.

When the light of knowledge reveals the seer as distinct from the seen, Sattva itself dissolves into pure consciousness.

The State Beyond the Guṇas

"He who, serving Me with unswerving devotion, transcends these three guṇas and becomes fit for Brahman."
— *Bhagavad Gita 14.26*

Shankara interprets this as the union of *Bhakti* and *Jñāna*. True devotion, he says, is abidance in the Self.
By resting in that awareness, the yogi transcends Sattva, Rajas, and Tamas, and abides as **Guṇātīta** — beyond the qualities.

In this freedom, the *guṇas* continue to play in the body and mind, but the Self remains untouched — the actor withdrawn from the stage yet witnessing the drama unfold.

Philosophical Summary: Guṇa Traya Vibhāga Yoga

Shankara's Advaitic synthesis:

- **The three guṇas** (Sattva, Rajas, Tamas) are the constituent forces of Nature.
- They bind the Self through identification with mind and body.
- **Sattva** purifies, **Rajas** agitates, **Tamas** obscures.
- Liberation comes by realizing that all *guṇas* belong to Prakṛti, not to the Self.
- The state of **Guṇātīta** is the stillness of pure awareness, beyond all opposites.

Thus, the yogi does not fight the *guṇas* but awakens from them, as one wakes from a dream.

Reflections for the Seeker

1. **Observe Without Judgment**
   Notice moods, impulses, and desires as movements of Nature. The witness is never altered.

2. **Cultivate Sattva but Do Not Cling**
   Let purity and clarity refine the mind, but know that even light must dissolve into the source of light.
3. **Abide as the Witness**
   When pleasure, restlessness, or dullness arise, remember: "These are guṇas; I am not these."
4. **Rest in the Self Alone**
   The moment you stop identifying with tendencies, you stand free—silent, radiant, untouched.

Conclusion: Beyond the Weave of Nature

For **Ādi Shankaracharya**, *Guṇa Traya Vibhāga Yoga* is **the psychology of liberation**.

To know the *guṇas* is to understand the machinery of bondage; to stand apart from them is to taste freedom itself.

When consciousness ceases to mistake the play for the player, it awakens as the timeless spectator of existence — beyond light and dark, beyond joy and sorrow, beyond the very pulse of Nature.

"When the lamp of Sattva burns itself out,
when Rajas and Tamas fall away,
there remains the light that needs no fuel—
the Self, eternal and serene."
— *Adi Shankaracharya*

The Yoga of the Supreme Self

The Ashvattha tree, with roots above and branches below, whose leaves are the Vedic hymns—he who knows this tree knows the Veda.
— *Bhagavad Gita 15.1*

The Cosmic Tree of Life

In this luminous chapter, Krishna describes the entire universe as an **inverted tree** (*Ashvattha*): its roots above in the immortal Brahman, its branches below in the world of change.

For **Ādi Shankaracharya**, this allegory captures **the nature of Samsāra itself** — the reflection of reality in illusion.

The roots above signify the eternal source, while the downward-spreading branches represent names and forms sustained by desire and karma.

To know the tree is to see its structure; to be free from it is to **sever its bondage with the sword of detachment**.

"The tree of the world is sustained by ignorance;
cut it down by the knowledge that you are not of it."
— *Shankara, Gita Bhāṣya 15.3*

The Inverted Order of Reality

Shankara interprets the upside-down image as a profound metaphor:

The *Ashvattha* is **rooted in the Unmanifest**, but what we experience is its **inversion**, like a reflection in water.

Thus, all perception is **reversed**—the unreal appears real, and the Real remains unseen.

To awaken is to invert perception again, seeing the world not as substance but as **appearance within consciousness**.

This is the essence of *Vedantic renunciation*—not escape from the world, but recognition of its dependent reality.

Detachment: The Sword of Wisdom

"With the strong sword of detachment, cut down this deeply rooted tree;

then seek that state from which there is no return."

— *Bhagavad Gita 15.3–4*

Shankara explains that detachment (*Vairāgya*) here is not withdrawal from life but **withdrawal of belief** in the world's absoluteness.

Actions continue, but attachment ceases; experiences arise, but identification dissolves.

When the root of ignorance is cut, the seeker ascends beyond the branches of karma into the **sky of the imperishable Self**.

The Supreme Abode

Krishna says:

"Neither sun nor moon nor fire illumines that place;

having gone there, none return."

— *Bhagavad Gita 15.6*

Shankara calls this *the luminous Self beyond duality*.

It is not a spatial realm but **the state of realization itself**—the awareness that shines by its own light.

The sun, moon, and fire symbolize borrowed illumination—knowledge that depends on objects.

The Supreme Light is **self-luminous consciousness**, the *Ātman*, which illumines all knowledge yet is illumined by none.

The Two Puruṣas: Perishable and Imperishable

Krishna distinguishes between two kinds of *Puruṣa* (spirit):

1. **Kṣara Puruṣa** — the perishable, embodied being, subject to change;
2. **Akṣara Puruṣa** — the imperishable Self, unchanging within all beings.

Then He reveals a third principle:

"Beyond both the perishable and the imperishable,
I am the Supreme Person (*Puruṣottama*),
sustaining the worlds and transcending them all."
— *Bhagavad Gita 15.17*

Shankara interprets this as **the culmination of Advaita**.

The *Puruṣottama* is not a third entity apart from the two but the **substratum of both**—the Reality in which both the changing and unchanging aspects appear.

It is Brahman viewed simultaneously as *Immanent* and *Transcendent*.

Thus, the perishable world, the imperishable Self, and the Supreme Consciousness are **one continuum of awareness**, seen at different levels of understanding.

The Self as the Source of Consciousness

"I am seated in the hearts of all; from Me come memory, knowledge, and their loss."
— *Bhagavad Gita 15.15*

Shankara explains that the Lord within is **the consciousness that enables every act of knowing and remembering**.

Mind and intellect are instruments; awareness alone is the light that animates them.

The Supreme Self is therefore not apart from human consciousness but **its very essence**.

To recognize this is to end the search for God outside oneself.

Cutting Through Reflection

Shankara offers a final insight:

The world-tree is *Ashvattha*, "not lasting even till tomorrow."

All experiences, joys, and sorrows are shadows cast by the eternal.

To cling to them is to live in reflection; to wake to the source is to live in freedom.

Detachment here is **not denial but discernment**—the understanding that only the witnessing awareness is real.

Philosophical Summary: Puruṣottama Yoga

Shankara's Advaitic synthesis:

- **The Ashvattha tree** symbolizes the reflected universe sustained by ignorance.
- **Cutting it down** means severing identification with the transient through discernment.
- **Kṣara** (perishable) = body-mind; **Akṣara** (imperishable) = witness consciousness.
- **Puruṣottama** transcends both as the one undivided Reality.
- **Liberation** is abiding as that awareness from which all arises and into which all returns.

Thus, realization of the Supreme Person is the recognition that **the Self of the individual and the Self of the universe are one**.

Reflections for the Seeker

1. **Contemplate the Cosmic Tree**
   See how all thoughts, forms, and desires grow from a single root—awareness. Trace them back to their source.
2. **Sever Identification**
   The sword of knowledge is not aggression but insight: "I am not the body, not the mind— I am the witness of both."
3. **Seek the Light Beyond All Lights**
   The ultimate illumination is not from the world but from the Self. Abide there.
4. **Worship the Inner Lord**
   To know Puruṣottama is to bow inwardly to the consciousness that animates all.

Conclusion: The Supreme Self Revealed

For **Ādi Shankaracharya**, *Puruṣottama Yoga* is the **crown of discernment**—the recognition of the Supreme Self as both the essence and the transcendent ground of all. When the inverted tree of illusion is cut, what remains is the clear sky of pure awareness.

There is no longer "above" or "below," "within" or "without"—only the vast stillness of the Self, radiant and self-knowing.

"When the roots of illusion are cut by knowledge,
the tree of becoming withers;
what remains is the rootless Reality,
the Puruṣottama, beyond all pairs and parts."
— *Adi Shankaracharya*

The Division Between the Divine and Demonic Nature

Fearlessness, purity of heart, steadfastness in knowledge and yoga,
charity, control of the senses, sacrifice, study, austerity, and straightforwardness—
these are the marks of the divine nature.
— *Bhagavad Gita 16.1–3*

The Inner Battlefield of Character

After revealing the Supreme Self (*Puruṣottama*), Krishna turns to the **psychological landscape** within which realization or bondage unfolds.
The sixteenth chapter maps the *forces of light and darkness* that dwell in every heart.

For **Ādi Shankaracharya**, this is not a moral sermon but a **spiritual anatomy**: the *Daivī Sampad* (divine endowment) are tendencies that lead the mind toward Self-knowledge; the *Āsurī Sampad* (demonic endowment) are impulses that entangle consciousness in ignorance.

"The divine qualities purify the intellect and make it fit for knowledge;
the demonic qualities thicken ignorance and bind the seeker to the field."
— *Shankara, Gita Bhāṣya 16.5*

The Divine Qualities: The Movement Toward Clarity

Krishna lists virtues such as serenity, compassion, humility, and faith in the scriptures.
Shankara interprets these as **reflections of Sattva Guṇa**—expressions of a mind that has turned inward toward the Self.

Divine nature is not inherited or bestowed; it is **cultivated through discipline and understanding**.
As knowledge deepens, these virtues arise spontaneously—like fragrance from a flower.

A person established in Daivī Sampad lives lightly, free from compulsion, acting from wisdom rather than impulse.

The Demonic Qualities: The Veil of Ignorance

"Hypocrisy, arrogance, self-conceit, anger, harshness, and ignorance—
these are the marks of the demonic."
— *Bhagavad Gita 16.4*

Shankara explains that *Āsurī Sampad* arises from **identification with ego and body**.
The demonic person is not a mythical being but the ordinary mind ruled by desire, pride, and fear.

Such a one, deluded by *Rajas* and *Tamas*, denies the moral order (*Dharma*) and the Self beyond the body.
He mistakes pleasure for fulfillment and possession for power, revolving endlessly in the cycle of craving and frustration.

The Root of the Demonic: Denial of the Self

"The demonic say: the world has no truth, no moral basis, no God;
it is born of desire alone."
— *Bhagavad Gita 16.8*

Shankara calls this the **philosophy of darkness**—the complete forgetting of the witness.
When consciousness identifies entirely with the body, it becomes blind to its own light.
From this blindness grow greed, violence, and fear.

The *Āsurī* mind seeks security through accumulation, unaware that its insecurity comes from ignorance, not scarcity.

Desire as the Chain of Bondage

Krishna describes the demonic man as driven by insatiable desire, convinced that he himself is the doer and enjoyer.
Shankara interprets this as the **root illusion of doership** (*Kartṛtvābhimāna*).
Until this notion dissolves, the mind remains bound to the results of its own actions.

"Desire, anger, and greed are the triple gate to hell;
therefore one should renounce them."
— *Bhagavad Gita 16.21*

Shankara comments: these three are but different shades of ignorance—*Desire* binds through longing, *Anger* through resistance, *Greed* through restlessness.
To abandon them is to return to the stillness of the Self.

Freedom Through Knowledge

"Freed from these three gates of darkness,
a man acts for his own liberation and not for bondage."
— *Bhagavad Gita 16.22*

Shankara clarifies that liberation here is not gained through moral purification alone, but through **knowledge illumined by virtue**.

When the intellect becomes pure, knowledge of Brahman arises naturally; the demonic tendencies simply lose their foundation.

Thus, virtue is not an end in itself but **the environment in which wisdom flowers**.

Faith and the Inner Compass

Krishna concludes by noting that those of divine nature act with faith in Dharma, while those of demonic nature follow blind impulse.

Shankara interprets faith (*Śraddhā*) as **trust in the truth of the Self** and reverence for the means that reveal it.

Without this trust, even good actions lose their transforming power.

Faith is therefore the bridge between moral discipline and spiritual realization.

Philosophical Summary: Daiva Āsura Sampad Vibhāga Yoga

Shankara's Advaitic interpretation may be distilled thus:

- **Daivī Sampad** leads the mind toward Sattva and knowledge of the Self.
- **Āsurī Sampad** binds through ego, ignorance, and desire.
- The battle between divine and demonic is **internal**, not cosmic.
- Moral purity prepares the intellect; knowledge consummates it.
- Transcending both virtue and vice, one abides as the Self, untouched by the play of qualities.

Virtue is the ladder, knowledge the ascent, freedom the summit.

Reflections for the Seeker

1. **Discern Inner Tendencies**
   Notice which thoughts uplift and which obscure; both are movements within the same consciousness.
2. **Cultivate Sattva**
   Simplicity, moderation, and truthfulness clear the mirror of the mind.
3. **Renounce the Triple Bond**
   Let go of desire, anger, and greed—not by suppression but by understanding their root in ignorance.
4. **Let Faith Mature into Knowledge**
   Believe first in the possibility of freedom; then realize it by seeing the Self as the only reality.

Conclusion: The Moral Order Within

For **Ādi Shankaracharya**, *Daiva Āsura Sampad Vibhāga Yoga* is a mirror in which the seeker perceives the mind's own duality.

The "divine" is not inherited divinity, and the "demonic" is not external evil—both are **currents of the same mind**.

When knowledge dawns, even these distinctions fade.

The true victory of the divine is not conquest over others but awakening within oneself.

"When the mind is illumined by knowledge,
virtue and vice lose meaning;
what remains is the Self—
pure, free, and complete."
— *Adi Shankaracharya*

The Division of Threefold Faith

The faith of every man conforms to his nature, O Bharata.
Faith is inherent in each; he is what his faith is.
— *Bhagavad Gita 17.3*

The Subtle Power of Faith

After distinguishing the divine and demonic natures, Krishna turns to the quiet but decisive force that shapes them both — **Śraddhā**, or faith.

For **Ādi Shankaracharya**, faith is not blind belief; it is **the orientation of the mind**, the inner conviction that propels action and understanding. It determines what we value, what we worship, and ultimately **what we become aware of as reality**.

"Faith is the seed from which knowledge or ignorance grows; as is the faith, so is the fruit."
— *Shankara, Gita Bhāṣya 17.3*

Faith and the Three Guṇas

Krishna reveals that faith, like all mental tendencies, arises under the influence of the three guṇas — **Sattva**, **Rajas**, and **Tamas**.

Shankara explains that faith is the **mirror of one's dominant guṇa**:

- **Sāttvic faith** reflects clarity and reverence for truth.
- **Rājasic faith** seeks power, pleasure, or reward.
- **Tāmasic faith** clings to ignorance, superstition, and inertia.

Just as water takes the color of the vessel that holds it, so faith takes the hue of the mind that contains it.

Sāttvic Faith — The Path of Clarity

"The sāttvic, worshipping the gods,
are disciplined in mind and heart."
— *Bhagavad Gita 17.4*

Shankara describes sāttvic faith as **purified trust** — devotion directed toward the higher Self, the essence of all deities. It leads to peace, discernment, and spontaneous compassion. Acts performed in sāttvic faith are free from compulsion; they are expressions of understanding, not bargaining with destiny.

This is the faith that matures into knowledge — the calm certainty that all is sustained by one consciousness.

Rājasic Faith — The Path of Desire

"The rājasic, seeking success and enjoyment,
worship the yakṣas and rākṣasas."
— *Bhagavad Gita 17.4*

Shankara interprets this symbolically: the *yakṣas* and *rākṣasas* represent **ambitious and restless forces** within the psyche. Rājasic faith is action-driven — it believes in effort but remains bound to results.

Even devotion becomes transactional: "I worship that I may obtain." Such faith, though more dynamic than tamas, is still a movement within bondage — the ego seeking permanence in the impermanent.

Tāmasic Faith — The Path of Delusion

"The tāmasic, enveloped in darkness,
worship spirits and ghosts; they follow irrational vows."
— *Bhagavad Gita 17.4*

For Shankara, this represents **blind faith without understanding** — rituals performed without awareness of purpose, austerities that harm oneself or others, or superstitions that replace insight with fear.

This form of faith is not spiritual power but spiritual inertia. It mistakes intensity for depth, form for truth, and suffering for sanctity.

The Threefold Division in Practice

Krishna extends the threefold division to **food, sacrifice, austerity, and charity** — showing that even these everyday acts reflect one's inner nature.

Shankara comments:

- **Sāttvic acts** purify and illumine;
- **Rājasic acts** agitate through desire for fruit;
- **Tāmasic acts** degrade through ignorance or neglect.

The wise therefore do not merely choose *what* to do but **from what consciousness** they do it.

The Ideal of Balance

Krishna describes *Tapas* (austerity) in three forms — of body, speech, and mind — emphasizing gentleness, truth, and self-restraint.

Shankara reminds that *Tapas* is not mortification but **refinement**. Its purpose is to quiet the senses so that knowledge may shine.

The sāttvic ascetic acts without ostentation, with faith in the Self as the witness of all discipline.

The Role of the Sacred Syllables: Om, Tat, Sat

"Om, Tat, and Sat — this is the triple designation of Brahman."
— *Bhagavad Gita 17.23*

Shankara gives profound symbolic meaning:

- **Om** — the sound-symbol of the Absolute, affirming the unity of existence.
- **Tat** — "That," indicating surrender of ego and the offering of all acts to the Supreme.
- **Sat** — truth and being, signifying what is real and enduring.

All sacred acts become sāttvic when performed in the spirit of *Om Tat Sat*:
awareness of unity, detachment from fruits, and alignment with truth.

Philosophical Summary: Śraddhā Traya Vibhāga Yoga

Shankara's Advaitic interpretation:

- **Śraddhā** is the mind's orientation — its faith in the real or unreal.
- The **three guṇas** shape the quality of faith and, through it, destiny.
- **Sāttvic faith** leads to knowledge; **Rājasic faith** sustains restlessness; **Tāmasic faith** deepens ignorance.
- All acts, when consecrated with *Om Tat Sat*, are purified of ego and aligned with truth.
- Ultimate faith is faith in the Self — the one consciousness underlying all beliefs.

Reflections for the Seeker

1. **Examine the Source of Your Faith**
   Is it born of fear, ambition, or clarity? That question reveals your guṇa.
2. **Transform Devotion Into Understanding**
   Let faith evolve from emotional reliance to intuitive knowing of the Self.
3. **Consecrate Every Act**
   Begin and end with awareness — *Om Tat Sat* — so that action becomes offering.
4. **Let Faith Mature Into Silence**
   When faith becomes direct seeing, belief dissolves in realization.

Conclusion: The Alchemy of Faith

For **Ādi Shankaracharya**, *Śraddhā Traya Vibhāga Yoga* shows that **liberation begins not with knowledge but with the capacity to believe in knowledge**.
Faith, rightly placed, turns inward and reveals its own source — the Self that never doubted.

When the guṇas are transcended and faith returns to its origin, it is no longer belief but **being**.

"Faith purified by understanding becomes knowledge;
knowledge realized as the Self becomes freedom;
freedom known as one's own nature becomes peace eternal."
— *Adi Shankaracharya*

The Yoga of Liberation and Renunciation

The wise call renunciation the giving up of actions born of desire;
the abandoning of all fruit of action, the learned call relinquishment.
— *Bhagavad Gita 18.2*

The Final Inquiry: What Is True Renunciation?

Arjuna begins this last discourse with a question that has echoed through all spiritual traditions:

"What is the difference between *Sannyāsa* (renunciation) and *Tyāga* (relinquishment)?"

For **Ādi Shankaracharya**, this question is not merely ethical — it is existential.
It asks: *What must one truly give up to be free?*

Shankara clarifies that **renunciation is not of action but of attachment**, not of work but of the sense of doership (*Kartṛtvābhimāna*).
Actions continue, but the actor dissolves.

"He who performs necessary duties without attachment to their fruits,

he alone is truly renounced, not he who abandons action itself."
— *Shankara, Gita Bhāṣya 18.9*

The Twofold Path: Knowledge and Action

Krishna harmonizes the seeming opposition between **Jñāna Yoga** and **Karma Yoga**.
He teaches that for the purified intellect, **renunciation and selfless action merge**.

Shankara explains:

- For the seeker still purifying the mind, action performed without selfish motive (*Nishkāma Karma*) is the means.
- For the knower established in Self-awareness, **renunciation arises spontaneously** — for what remains to be done by one who sees all as Self?

Thus, renunciation is the natural fragrance of wisdom.

The Threefold Nature of Action

"Knowledge, action, and the doer are declared to be threefold, according to the distinction of the guṇas."
— *Bhagavad Gita 18.19*

Shankara analyzes this triad deeply:

- **Sāttvic knowledge** sees the one imperishable Self in all beings.
- **Rājasic knowledge** perceives separateness — a world of distinctions.
- **Tāmasic knowledge** mistakes the transient for the eternal.

Similarly, the **doer** may act with purity and balance (Sattva), with greed and restlessness (Rajas), or with delusion and negligence (Tamas).

The goal is not to destroy these tendencies but to **see through them** — to know that the Self is never the doer at all.

The Witness Beyond Action

Krishna declares:

"The Lord dwells in the hearts of all beings,
causing them to revolve by His power, as if mounted on a machine."
— *Bhagavad Gita 18.61*

Shankara's commentary here is luminous:
The *machine* is the body-mind mechanism; the *power* is Prakṛti; and the *Lord* is the witnessing consciousness, unattached yet enabling all.

To mistake the machinery for the Self is bondage;
to recognize oneself as the unmoved witness is freedom.

"Action belongs to Nature;
seeing this, the wise neither act nor refrain, but rest in Being."
— *Shankara, Gita Bhāṣya 18.17*

The Role of Knowledge in Liberation

Knowledge (*Jñāna*) alone, says Shankara, **cuts the knot of ignorance** that ties consciousness to the body.
No ritual, austerity, or pilgrimage can achieve what one flash of insight accomplishes: the recognition that *I am not the doer, nor the enjoyer — I am the eternal witness of both.*

Such knowledge is not acquired; it is uncovered. The Self was never bound — only mistaken.

The Highest Devotion

"By devotion he comes to know Me truly;
and knowing Me, he enters into Me."
— *Bhagavad Gita 18.55*

Shankara harmonizes *Bhakti* and *Jñāna* here: true devotion is **love of truth**, and true knowledge is **the fulfillment of love**.

When duality dissolves, devotion becomes identity — the knower and the known are one.

Thus, **Bhakti culminates in Advaita**, and **Advaita blossoms as Bhakti**.

The Divine Command: Surrender of the Ego

"Abandon all dharmas and take refuge in Me alone;
I will liberate thee from all sins — do not grieve."
— *Bhagavad Gita 18.66*

This verse, *the Gita's heart and crown*, is interpreted by Shankara as the **supreme declaration of Advaita**.
"Abandoning all dharmas" means letting go of all limited notions — of duty, identity, and even the idea of striving for liberation.

To "take refuge in Me" is to rest as **the Self itself** — pure consciousness, beyond all attributes.
Sins and bondage are only misunderstandings; when knowledge arises, they vanish like mist before the sun.

"Refuge in Me" is not an act, but the recognition
that there is no other refuge apart from the Self.
— *Shankara, Gita Bhāṣya 18.66*

The Peace of Fulfillment

Krishna concludes by asking Arjuna whether his delusion has been destroyed.
Arjuna answers:

"Destroyed is my delusion, O Achyuta!
Through Thy grace, I have regained remembrance.
I stand firm; my doubt is gone."
— *Bhagavad Gita 18.73*

Shankara remarks that this symbolizes the end of ignorance (*Avidyā Nivṛtti*) — not the attainment of something new, but the unveiling of what always was.
The seeker does not become liberated; he **recognizes he was never bound**.

Philosophical Summary: Mokṣa Sannyāsa Yoga

Shankara's Advaitic synthesis:

- **Renunciation (Sannyāsa)** is the relinquishment of ego and the fruits of action.
- **Knowledge (Jñāna)** reveals the Self as non-doer and non-enjoyer.
- **Devotion (Bhakti)** matures into identity with the Supreme.
- **Surrender (Śaraṇāgati)** is not external but inner dissolution of separateness.
- **Liberation (Mokṣa)** is the natural state of the Self — timeless, self-luminous, complete.

Thus, the Gita's eighteen chapters culminate not in doctrine, but in silence — the stillness of understanding.

Reflections for the Seeker

1. **Act Without Ownership**
   Let life unfold through you, not from you. The Self is the witness, not the worker.
2. **Let Knowledge End Effort**
   Freedom is not earned — it is remembered. Stop seeking and simply see.
3. **Offer All into Awareness**
   Every thought and act dissolves when seen as movement in consciousness.
4. **Rest as the Self**
   Beyond all guṇas, beyond all dharmas, beyond all dualities — you are that.

Conclusion: The Silence of Liberation

For **Ādi Shankaracharya**, *Mokṣa Sannyāsa Yoga* is not the end of the *Gita*; it is the **end of becoming**.

The battlefield fades, the dialogue ceases, and what remains is pure awareness — the listener, speaker, and teaching dissolved into one.

This is the state of *Jīvanmukti* — liberation while living — where the world continues to move, but the Self remains unmoved.

"When knowledge ripens into silence,
when action becomes effortless being,
when devotion dissolves into oneness —
that is Mokṣa."
— *Adi Shankaracharya*

Epilogue – The Timeless Voice of the Gita

Beyond Scripture, Into the Silence of the Self

Wherever there is Krishna, the Lord of Yoga,
and Arjuna, the disciple of the bow,
there is fortune, victory, and peace.
— *Bhagavad Gita 18.78*

The Eternal Dialogue

The *Bhagavad Gita* began with despair — a warrior trembling between duty and emotion, between the call of action and the ache of compassion.

It ends in illumination — the same warrior, now still within, seeing the same battlefield as an expression of the Self.

For **Ādi Shankaracharya**, this transformation is the essence of *Vedānta*:

the movement from **ignorance to insight**, from **duality to unity**, from **struggle to serenity**.

What began as dialogue between Krishna and Arjuna becomes the **conversation between the finite and the infinite** — between the restless mind and the witnessing consciousness.

And when understanding dawns, both voices merge into one — the knower and the known are seen as the same.

The Gita as Mirror of the Self

Shankara saw the *Gita* not as a religious book, but as a **mirror for inquiry**.

Its verses do not command belief — they awaken seeing.

Each teaching, when reflected upon, turns the seeker inward from the outer battlefield to the **inner field of awareness**.

The *Gita*, he says, is a **scripture of realization** (*Anubhava Śāstra*).

Its words are not ends in themselves; they are lamps that dissolve in their own light.

Once knowledge is direct, the need for instruction ceases — just as the finger pointing to the moon is forgotten when the moon is seen.

From Conflict to Clarity

In Shankara's interpretation, every chapter represents a stage of evolution:

- The first — *Vishāda Yoga* — begins with crisis, the trembling of ego before truth.
- The middle chapters unfold disciplines — of knowledge, devotion, and discrimination.
- The final chapters dissolve all distinctions into the stillness of the Self.

The *Gita* thus traces the **spiritual physiology** of awakening — the gradual refinement of the intellect until it becomes transparent to the Self.

"When the mind is purified by knowledge and devotion,
it becomes like a clear crystal reflecting the light of Brahman."
— *Shankara*

Shankara's Legacy: Advaita in Motion

Through the lens of **Advaita Vedānta**, Shankara restored the *Gita* to its core message:
that the ultimate reality is one — **Brahman**, pure consciousness —
and that liberation (*Mokṣa*) is nothing other than **recognition of this truth**.

For him, the *Gita* is not a call to external renunciation but to **inner detachment amid engagement**.
Action continues, but it becomes *Līlā* — divine play.
Knowledge dawns, but it is not intellectual — it is being aware that awareness alone is real.

The Modern Seeker and the Ancient Song

Though spoken in a battlefield ages ago, the *Gita*'s voice speaks to every moment of decision in modern life.
To the physician, it whispers: *Heal without ownership.*
To the entrepreneur: *Create without greed.*
To the artist: *Express without ego.*
To the restless mind: *Be still and know that you are the witness of all.*

Shankara's insights bridge the ancient and the contemporary — showing that spirituality is not escape, but clarity within complexity.
The battlefield today may be psychological, social, or digital — yet the wisdom remains the same: *Act, but do not attach; love, but do not cling; know, and be free.*

The Silence Beyond Words

Every scripture ends where truth begins — in silence.
As Shankara wrote, "The Self cannot be taught; it is realized when teaching ends."

When the seeker stops searching for peace as an object and recognizes peace as the nature of the Self,
when the opposites of action and renunciation dissolve,

when 'I' and 'Thou' become one luminous stillness —
the *Gita* completes itself.

"The song of the Lord is not in sound but in silence —
the silence that hears all songs."
— *Adi Shankaracharya*

The Closing Benediction

May this work serve not as doctrine but as **illumination** —
a companion for the intellect and a compass for the soul.

May the reader, like Arjuna, rise from the field of confusion to the height of clarity —
not to conquer others, but to **realize the invincible peace within**.

And may the voice of Krishna, as interpreted by Shankara, continue to echo in every heart that seeks truth not as belief, but as being.

About the Author

Dr Surabhi Solanki is a lifelong student of Indian philosophy with a deep passion for bringing timeless wisdom into the modern world. Drawn early to the transformative teachings of the *Bhagavad Gita* and the clarity of Adi Shankaracharya's commentaries, she has spent years studying Vedanta, classical Sanskrit texts, and the historical contexts that shaped India's spiritual traditions.

With a background in both scholarly research and contemporary writing, the author focuses on making ancient knowledge accessible without losing its depth. Her work blends scriptural insight with practical reflection, helping readers engage with the *Gita* not only as a spiritual text but as a guide for meaningful living.

This book, *Bhagavad Gita: Insights from Adi Shankaracharya*, reflects Dr Surabhi's commitment to honouring tradition while illuminating its relevance today. Through careful interpretation and thoughtful analysis, she invites readers to explore the essence of non-duality, the nature of the Self, and the path to inner freedom—core ideas championed by Shankaracharya.

Other works by the author include:

Divine Truth Unveiled: Hidden Secrets of Gaudapada's Mandukya Karika;

Essence of Yoga Vasistha: The Book of Liberation;

Power Beyond Perception: Modern Insights into the Kena Upanishad;

Awakening Through Vedanta: Timeless Wisdom of Adi Shankaracharya;

The Hidden Secrets of Immortality: Katha Upanishad Retold;

Brahma Sutra Bhashya: A Modern Retelling.

Official Website: drsurabhisolanki.com

Email: drsurabhisolanki@gmail.com

9 789356 192645

Printed at Repro India Ltd.